THE MODERN JEWISH TABLE

100 KOSHER RECIPES FROM AROUND THE GLOBE

TRACEY FINE *and* GEORGIE TARN
THE JEWISH PRINCESSES

Skyhorse Publishing
A Herman Graf Book

Skyhorse Publishing books may be purchased in bulk at special discounts for sales promotion, corporate gifts, fund-raising, or educational purposes. Special editions can also be created to specifications. For details, contact the Special Sales Department, Skyhorse Publishing, 307 West 36th Street, 11th Floor, New York, NY 10018 or info@skyhorsepublishing.com.

Skyhorse® and Skyhorse Publishing® are registered trademarks of Skyhorse Publishing, Inc.®, a Delaware corporation.

Visit our website at www.skyhorsepublishing.com.

10 9 8 7 6 5 4 3 2 1

Library of Congress Cataloging-in-Publication Data is available on file.

Although all reasonable care has been taken in the preparation of this book, neither the publisher, editor(s) nor the authors can accept any liability for any consequences arising from the use thereof, or the information contained therein.

Cover design by Jenny Zemanek
Cover photo credit by Rupa Photography London

Photography and production by Rupa Photography London
Art direction by Mandy Thompson
Food and prop styling by Mandy Thompson

Print ISBN: 978-1-5107-1718-3
Ebook ISBN: 978-1-5107-1719-0

Printed in China

TABLE OF CONTENTS

Red Cabbage, Beet & Apple Borscht   45
Sephardi Saffron Chicken Soup with Fragrant Matzo Balls   47
Sweetcorn Chowder   49
Vietnamese Vegetarian Pho Soup   51
Yemenite Meat Soup   52
Watercress Soup   53

SALADS—GO GREEN   55

Adzuki, Wasabi & Bell Pepper Salad   58
Bejeweled Sweet Potato, Beet & Pomegranate Salad   59
Brie Pear & Caramelized Walnuts on Endive Leaves   61
Carrot, Coconut & Ginger Salad   62
Horseradish New Potato Salad   63
Roasted Celery Root Salad   64
Roasted Red Bell Pepper & Tuna Salad with Sherry Vinegar   65
Sharon Persimmon Fruit & Sugar Snap Pea Salad   67
Warm Jerusalem Salad   69
Tomato Gazpacho Salad   70

FISH WITH NO FINGERS   71

Baked Salmon Fish Cakes with Polenta Fries   75
Fish Blintzes   77
Mexican Salmon Ceviche   80
Sea Bass with Salse Verde   81
Sea Bream Stew   82
Street Food Gefilte Fish Bites   83
Stuffed Coconut Rainbow Trout   85
Sun-Blushed Tomato & Artichoke-Crusted Loin of Cod   86
Quick Fish Pâté   87
Tuna Tataki   88

CAKE—A SLICE OF HEAVEN   149

COOKIES & TINY TREATS THAT TAKE THE BISCUIT   167

COUTURE CHOCOLATE   185

DEDICATION

We dedicate this book to our beautiful, amazing, talented, wonderful, and clever children; after all, they take after their mothers.

Please don't feel any Jewish Guilt (even though we worried about you from the moment we thought of having you). When you eventually arrived by the power of the Caesarean section, we finally understood the meaning of the word *neurotic*. Nine months and counting we spent carrying you, sacrificing our tight butts and other areas of our bodies, which we won't mention, but we assure you it was well worth it. We will never again know a night of uninterrupted beauty sleep; but if you could try and not mislay your keys at 4:00 a.m., we would be most grateful.

Remember, we are *not* pushy parents—it's not a push, just a little shove in the right direction.

We will always be there for you, even when we are traveling the world. We promise there will always be chicken soup in the freezer, **kneidlach**, spare **lokshen**, and, of course, a roast chicken or two.

One day when you are married to a doctor, a lawyer, or an accountant (we are not fussy), and when you have children, who will grow up to be doctors, lawyers, or accountants, know that we may *not* be available for babysitting duties, because we will be in Florida playing golf. But don't worry, you are always welcome to visit; we hear they have wonderful hotels!

Keep this book as a token of our adoration and affection. Remember that food is a gift of love. When we are old and gray (scratch that!) and look younger than our years, still strutting our stuff in our heels even with designer Zimmer frames, please follow these recipes. We shall **shep naches** with every delicious mouthful we eat. We will boast to all our friends, neighbors, relatives, and strangers that you take after your mothers and that you truly are amazing cooks, with the style, panache, and ability to make it all look so easy.

We adore you all equally. You are our **bubbelahs**, our everything, our true successes.

Our wonderful and amazing Jewish Prince and Princesses.

Kneidlach: Dumpling

Lokshen: Noodles

Shep naches: Taking great pride and pleasure

Bubbelahs: Term of endearment, especially for children

Tracey's bubbelahs: Max Fine, Honey Fine

Georgie's bubbelahs: Cassie Tarn, Eden Tarn, Darcy Tarn

INTRODUCTION

We have something to confess, and this isn't our handbag habit.
We are the Jewish Princesses, and we are foodies.

Culinary creativity turns us on; it gets our juices flowing. When we enter the kitchen, we transform into Agent Provocateurs, Femme Fatales, Feeders—whipping, beating, tasting, and creating food fantasies. We don't have to be chained to the kitchen sink to produce culinary masterpieces, shame. The pleasure of getting down and dirty (but not that dirty) unleashes our passion. We admit it, we have been indulging in too much Mommy Porn, Fifty Shades of **Oy Vey**!

We live our lives in search of fabulous recipes. You can find us in gourmet restaurants or at the local café. We are not fussy; we just love food. We eat food, dream food, and think about food—as we are cooking food. We are always on a mission to seek out top-notch fresh ingredients, delicacies, and new flavors to tantalize our taste buds. We look to both vintage and contemporary ideas for inspiration. We study Jewish history, delighting in the treasure trove of wonderful foods that have been handed down from generation to generation, emanating from all over the Jewish **diaspora—Sephardic, Ashkenazi, Mizrahi**. Amazing culinary jewels like Yemenite Meat Soup (page 52) and Persian Sultana Brown Rice (page 120) are just a few examples to whet your appetite.

Within these golden pages you will learn our kitchen secrets (the bedroom ones will have to wait). Learn how to lay your table in preparation for Jewish small plates, sensational soups, salads, main-event meats, vegetarian entrees, and **pareve** desserts, as well as a whole chapter devoted to our favorite scholarly subject, chocolate, which we have always excelled in. We have tested, tasted, and sampled dishes from classic to current. These recipes are modern, chic, a la mode, hip hop and happening, and they will set your kitchen on fire (not literally, we hope).

So, no excuses: get out your KitchenAid®, plug in your vibrator, we mean your blender, and sharpen your tools, because we are Zumba-ing into your life, with wonderful foods plus a pinch of *chutzpah*. After all, when it comes to being the Jewish Princesses, it's not just chopped liver and chicken soup that is on the menu.

—Tracey Fine and Georgie Tarn

Oy Vey: dismay

Diaspora: The historical dispersion of the Jews

Sephardic: A Jewish person from Spanish or Portuguese descent

Ashkenazi: A Jewish person from Central or Eastern Europe

Mizrahi: A Jewish person from the Middle East

Pareve: Foods that contain no dairy products

Chutzpah: Cheek

WHAT TYPE OF COOK ARE YOU?

Welcome to the kitchen, the heart of the home, the place where we meet over a cup of tea (green, detox, energizer, make-me-go-to-sleep-now, or otherwise). It is where the past, present, and future can be found in a slice of cake, a bowl of soup, or an abundant fridge. However, there are so many different types of kitchens and styles of cooks, let's explore a few of our favorites:

RUSTIC FANTASTIC

Even if you don't have a house in the country, a chateau in France, or a finca in Spain, the Rustic Fantastic cook dreams of getting away from it all. They long for filled terra-cotta pots, an orange orchard, and picking their own produce, fruit, vegetables, and herbs (or maybe getting the gardener to do it!). They fancy eating breakfast, lunch, and candlelit dinners al fresco. They visualize the day when they can have their year in Provence. Even if it is just a dream, they still can't resist bringing the countryside into their home, even if it is a home in North West London, Long Island, or Boca Raton! (By the way, if you do own this dream abode, we are available *most* weekends!)

This type of cook can't help picking up pottery or stocking up on wooden chopping boards, and they certainly wouldn't dream of anything dainty; they love living life *large*. Their signature style in the kitchen is to use their hands to get down and dirty, producing peasant food with pizzazz and seasonal food that is sensational. They make everything seem so easy, and they don't like wasting their time busying themselves with the little details. What better way to serve a salad than by heaping it, country-pile-style, onto a large plate? Who needs to chop herbs when tearing them up is much more fun? Casseroles and slow cooking is a must, even if they don't own a country oven (one day, one day).

A Rustic Fantastic loves trying out new global flavors because they are always in holiday mode. Their pantry is filled with different exotic herbs and spices that sit snug alongside chutneys and home preserves (Whole Foods has fabulous options). They will love home stewing (see Spicy Fruit Salad, page 144). They are not put off by a bit of experimentation; in fact, fusion turns them on, or at least it turns their ovens on. However, you won't find a Rustic Fantastic going Michelin—it simply isn't simple enough. So, no nouveau for them.

If you are lucky enough to be invited to a Rustic Fantastic's dinner table, go hungry, as once they get cooking they just can't help but prepare a feast. With their bon vivant attitude, you won't be invited alone; after all, what better way to share good food and fantastic red wine by the case (imported from France) but with good friends? Be prepared for a crowd.

Even with their charming sense of style, a Rustic Fantastic can still stumble into the occasional pitfall. They simply get too carried away, resulting in far too many flavors that are mixed together in far too many dishes. Take note: even if your farmhouse-style table can seat ten, it doesn't mean you have to make ten dishes to choose from.

We would say we are a bit Rustic Fantastic. We get a kick out of seeing our friends and family diving into their meals, sharing and caring. We like to live large, and sometimes we don't have the patience or the time to measure, weigh, and finely dice.

So, if you feel a bit Rustic Fantastic and want to visit the countryside of cooking, think about what you are going to make and plan what is going to work well together, whether it's a hearty Lentil Soup (page 42), followed by a large bowl of Layered Provence Lamb (page 98), and a sensational Scottish Flapjack Berry Cobbler (page 143) to finish—all served in pottery, of course!

SILVER SERVICE

A Silver Service cook has style by the mile. They take great pride, care, and precision in everything they do. Neatness and order is paramount—they don't think it's strange to stock-take their pantry, ensuring that all pans are facing the same direction (woe betide anyone who moves them). In their ultra-modern minimal kitchen, usually white glossy, white matte, or simply stainless steel (which is absolutely impossible to clean), they will only have the most essential items on display, preferring even a hot tap to the mess of a kettle. The oven or any other gadgets they invest in will be the latest, greatest, computerized, high-tech pieces of equipment that only they can operate, as they have studied the manual back to front. The day robots become available, Silver Service will already be online to purchase one, but for the moment they will have to stick to their iPhones, dictating to Siri their to-do list, ticking off each task as soon as it is completed, or maybe using their own specially devised app. Anything is possible when you are Silver Service.

You may think this type of control and military precision would not make for a good cook, but if Silver Service decides to take the time and trouble, I can promise you they will be producing magnificent food. They are the Commander-in-Chief of their kitchen, unafraid to try out new flavors, as long as they have done their research to know exactly what they need, when they will need it, and how long each dish will take to prepare (they don't like to be rushed). When it comes to presentation, you will never find a smudge or a spot—everything will be as shiny and perfect as their white, sleek, expensive crockery. The food will look restaurant-worthy and taste superb. A Silver Service cook will deliver a first class treat on a perfectly starched tablecloth, and you will never be left waiting.

Desserts are a particular forté as their meticulous nature lends itself to the science and precision of baking. A Silver Service would be delighted to make our Macaroons or Macarons, the Real McCoy (page 180) or whisk up a Zabaglione with Ladyfingers (page 145), all made exactly with the same widths, lengths, and diameters.

We like to think we have a little Silver Service in us. We may not have the sleek white kitchen, and actually we don't have the Neiman Marcus dinner service (but we can dream). However, our cupboard shelves are pretty tidy, and when we are in the mood we can channel military pastry perfection (see our Choux Princess Pareve Profiteroles (page 136). However, we wouldn't always want to be a Silver Service as they can definitely veer toward being a little too OCD. Plus, admit it, we can't always be perfect!

Being a Silver Service cook is something one should aspire to be from time to time. In our opinion, there is nothing wrong with raising one's standards to use a little more precision, formality, and modernity, as long as it is still accompanied by that vital ingredient—warmth. As for getting to know our ovens (and we apologize that we haven't managed to buy a steam oven *yet*), we have to admit: we wouldn't have a clue how to use one.

THE HEALTH NUT

My body is my temple, my kitchen is my workout. I only eat clean food (what does that mean, actually?), and all the ingredients I use are organic and GMO-free. These are the sorts of statements you will hear from The Health Nut.

When you walk or jog into The Health Nut's kitchen, you will immediately notice their top-of-the-range juicer to whizz up wicked green juices, their recycling bin, and maybe a few crystals placed around the room as advised by their personal Feng Shui guru. Their countertops will be lined with powders, potions, vitamin bottles, nuts, and seeds that are stored in air-tight jars, and they will have a library of self-help guides and a huge amount of healthy cookery books (they are always looking for a cake recipe that is gluten-free, dairy-free, and sugar-free that has no calories).

A Health Nut has to cook from scratch, no pre-made food *ever*! They generally cook well because food is so important to them. They are not going to have recipes like our Naughty Peanut Chocolate Fudge Brownies (page 198), unless they have hidden them somewhere for emergency cravings. But you will find fabulous fresh food. All your carbs will be complex, protein is usually poultry, fish or eggs will be light and flavorsome, and of course everything will be accompanied by a super-food salad, like our Warm Jerusalem Salad (page 69). You might even get a chance to eat foods you never knew existed. Have you tried spirulina?

The Health Nut has a wealth of nutritional information under his or her weight-lifting belt, and they are more than delighted to impart it—how many calories should be consumed per day, fat-to-muscle ratio, and how to achieve a six-pack. You might even receive a going home present, an eating plan, a pot of protein powder, and an exercise wall chart.

If invited over to the Health Nut's home, it will probably be a lunchtime invitation as the Health Nut likes to be in bed early to rejuvenate and study their Fitbit watch (which, if it doesn't register the right number of steps completed for the day, will get them hopping back out of bed again). If you arrive feeling tired (either post-workout or hung-over), don't worry, your colorful plate of food will do amazing things. It will be so fresh, organic, delicious, healthy, and nutritious, accompanied by water from the Andes infused with something, that you will probably walk out looking ten years younger. If you happen not to fancy what's on the menu, just say you have intolerances (they love that, most Health Nuts are intolerant of practically everything). The Health Nut won't get upset. After all, they are so positive, upbeat, and understanding (due to all the self-help guides) that they will be more than delighted to knock you up a glass of wicked green juice (you should think about saying yes to that one). Be prepared for dessert yoga, a mindfulness lecture, and eating very slowly, as each bite must be chewed at least twenty times!

We have a little bit of the Health Nut in us. We have reached a certain age where we are still not certain of anything, so we give everything a go. If eating healthily can turn back the hands of time, we will give it a try. It is really fun to challenge ourselves, and not just in a spinning class. We love creating new and exciting healthy recipes such as the Persian Sultana Brown Rice (page 120), especially once we have jogged around our local organic health-food stores to pick and choose from a variety of earthy flavors.

LOOK DON'T COOK

A Look Don't Cook loves cooking. The only problem is they don't actually cook themselves. They are culinary voyeurs, avidly reading about food in magazines, salivating their way through recipe books (well, have you seen the cake sections?). And they can't wait to tune into cookery shows.

A Look Don't Cook may appear to have a perfectly lovely and functional kitchen. If you look through the keyhole, the well-thumbed cookery books, a few gleaming gadgets (wedding presents), and gorgeous crockery and cutlery (wedding presents) might fool you. But look a little closer, and there are tell-tale signs. Take a peek in the pantry and you will find a huge variety of amazing unopened ingredients, for the one day they might give it "a go." If you make your way to the end drawer on the left, what will you find hidden away?

A stack of take-away and catering company pamphlets used on the occasional night a Look Don't Cook is *not* eating out.

With their great food appreciation, why is it that they are looking and not cooking? They are scared—petrified of getting it all wrong. Cooking just seems too difficult; why would they want to tear their hair out even trying? They have raised the bar so high watching, judging, and reading that actually doing it themselves seems like an ordeal they will put off for another day, perhaps next year. If you ask why, they will blame it on time—either they don't have time or can't make time (obviously watching TV takes no time at all). Or, if they did give it a go, they would get all the cooking timings wrong.

If you do get invited over, don't fall off your chair in shock. They might have said dinner, but just a couple of days before, as eggs is eggs, they will chicken out and it will be changed to drinks (go anyway, they serve fabulous champagne; *it's the guilt*). After which they will dash off to order from their favorite eatery.

We can't blame them; sometimes we are a bit of a Look Don't Cook. When we read articles, flick through recipe books, or watch the latest batch of contestants crying their eyes out as they stare into their oven because their cake has gone pear-shaped instead of apple-shaped, it can all seem too much like hard work.

A Look Don't Cook is so frustrating because they just need a bit of motivation to discover that actual cooking is far more rewarding and tasty than eating out or ordering in every night.

With a little help and encouragement, a Look Don't Cook can transform into the best cook of all. So, if you are thumbing through the latest cookbook (this one), maybe now is the time to don your apron.

Therefore, whether you are a Rustic Fantastic, a Silver Service, a Health Nut, a Look Don't Cook, or a combination of all of the above, one thing is true: we all love food and excellent recipes with fabulous flavors that never fail.

Our new book is a culinary "GPS" with flavors that will take you all over the world, showing you how to take the quickest route from A to B to get maximum results.

First step, turn right, go straight ahead, and open the pantry cabinet.

Let's get cooking!

SETTING YOUR TABLE

When entertaining, it's not only the host (you) who must look fabulous—when your guests set eyes on your table, they should know immediately that they are in for a real treat. The table sets the stage for all that is to follow. Therefore, we believe a little table magic is in order to add sparkle and illusion (and you don't need to be David Copperfield to have a few tricks up your sleeve). By adding the right lighting, cutlery, crockery, and table coverings, and using a little imagination, you can transform your event into a showstopper.

Laying a table is like putting on your makeup—you need to start with the foundation. Just as it is with your skin, protection is essential, so it is worth investing in a heatproof table pad. We know, it is a little **bubbe**-ish, but sometimes **bubbes** are right! Another trick handed down from our grandmothers is to lay the table a few days prior to an event. Your tablecloth must be crisply starched—just like your face, you don't want any wrinkles to show. One must check that it is placed evenly with no lumps and bumps. As for the size, make sure it has a good drop. If it's too small, it will look like it has shrunk in the wash; if you go full length, make sure it only just hits the floor—any longer and it could become a health and safety risk.

We don't all possess a huge range of tablecloths. So, to add some table couture, why not visit your local fabric shop and buy some materials? There are so many to choose from, and inspiration will hit you once you are in the store—just don't forget to take your table measurements with you. You can use pastel linens in the spring and gossamer layered over white in the summer. And for a winter wonderland, what could be more wonderful than voluptuous velvet? One can also layer with lace for a more romantic feel or use a black tablecloth with a red runner along the center to get in the Zen mood. The choices are endless.

A Princess-Perfect lint-free table takes it to the next level (five-star deluxe), so keep a lint roller on hand or sticky scotch tape to pick up any unwanted fluff or stray cotton. When it comes to napkins, you can go crazy with color or keep it cool and contemporary as long as they are cloth. Paper simply isn't Princess Posh; our advice is to break open a packet of paper napkins only when serving the family and not guests.

If you don't want to use a tablecloth, there are now an enormous variety of table mats on offer, everything from slate to wood. You can use these mats as building blocks to alternate color and texture. For example, use wood for each place setting, with black slate mats running down the center to keep your table free from the ring marks that are caused when glasses are set directly on the table; we are not talking about diamond rings here. To raise your game, you can always rent fabulous mirrored placemats; these reflect your hard work and provide a fairyland feel.

It's all about impact—creating drama, personality, theme, and style for an event. Just let your table become a world full of imagination. It doesn't always have to be silver service (though sometimes, it works!).

Here are some ideas to get you in the mood. Let us be your Jewish Princess personal stylists and give your table a makeover.

> **Bubbe:** A Jewish grandmother

A RUSTIC LUNCH OR BAGEL BRUNCH

Tablecloth and Napkins

Hessian material with complementary napkins, tied with twine, immediately transports your guests to the countryside. The color is up to you—oranges, greens, plums, and pinks for an orchard feel, or beiges and creams to conjure up a field of dreams. You can forage in the garden on the day of the event and gather large flat leaves or wild flowers to scatter over the table.

Cutlery

Gather your cutlery together and place them into terra-cotta plant pots at the center of the table for guests to help themselves. Interspersed with potted washed herbs, this will add edible excitement, and a few guests might even take a nibble.

Glassware and Crockery

Glasses and crockery can be an eclectic mix, which is fabulous if you haven't got enough of one set. It is always fun to hunt out unusual crockery and glass (and maybe a designer coat) at flea markets; it's always amazing what you can find. Okay, you might have to get up early to snag the good bargains, but that makes it all worthwhile.

Ideas for serving a rustic lunch

Use baskets, wooden chopping boards, and even old, recycled jam jars to serve condiments. Use glass bottles for juice and water. Once again, these objects can be placed in the middle of the table, allowing guests to help themselves.

PRINCESS TEA PARLOR

For an Alice in Wonderland flavor, do as the Mad Hatter and let your imagination run White Rabbit wild. Your inner Queen of Hearts will create an event that will make your guests grin like Cheshire Cats. It's all about playing with different sizes and colors—and having fun.

Tablecloth and Napkins

Go pastel gingham and choose from lemon, pink, apple green, and lilac. All look fresh and fabulous. Or how about a crisp white tablecloth, with red felt hearts of various sizes and playing cards scattered all over the table?

If you go online, you can find miniature milk bottles (Amazon has all the answers). In every one, place a flower, a napkin, and a sticker with each guest's name. Another idea is to fill the bottles with Alice's magic potion in keeping with the theme (we would like a potion that makes us a little taller). If you go down the second route, have no fear, Alice is here: tie each napkin with a giant bow made of satin.

Cutlery

Four o'clock is the perfect time to use pretty pastry forks, butter knives, and teaspoons. If you haven't got any on hand, there are some incredible choices you can find online or at antique fairs or your local charity shops. Our preferred option is to visit our mothers, the Queens of Hearts—they always have a treasure trove of items that they have gathered over the years.

To keep with the theme, display your cutlery in a clock-like fashion: for example, place the teaspoons one on top of each other, then fan them out, creating a circular face.

Cakes take center stage at a tea party, so hunt down some theatrical cake knives—they also make great birthday gifts (hint, hint). Bejeweled handles, crystals, and even a cake knife fashioned as a shoe are perfect choices for Princesses.

Tea Service

Delicate, dainty bone china is called for, and mismatched pieces are perfect for this theme—the madder, the better (think Christian Lacroix). Clash your oranges, reds, and pinks, and don't be afraid to make a statement. Forget placing tea cups on a saucer and remember the theme—some tea cups can be placed upside down, others on their side, and even underneath a saucer (see Alice's Topsy Turvy Teatime Treats, page 171).

Ideas for Serving an Alice in Wonderland Tea Party

Use a giant teapot or individual teapots. Take out your three-tier cake stands. If you haven't got any, it's time for a "clever craft" moment. Take a crystal drinking tumbler, turn it upside down, and stick a pretty plate on top (using Sticky Tack). Playing with heights adds another dimension to a Wonderland table.

COME DINE WITH ME

For a Posh Princess dinner party, our motto is, "If you've got it, flaunt it." Now is the time to bring out the family heirlooms and go for silver service, crystal, and candelabras. You can go as big as you want—the greater the impact, the better the drama. A little polishing may be required, but we never said you had to do it.

For any event after dark, it is a must to dine by candlelight, and it is up to the hostess with the mostess (that's you) to make sure the candles are lit before your guests enter. If you are going for scented candles, make sure they are all of the same scent (nothing too potent) or your guests will not be able to appreciate your delicious food after being overcome by perfume.

When inviting guests who don't know each other well, or if you have invited a fairly large number, knowing where your guests are going to sit makes your life and everybody else's a lot easier. There is nothing worse than stranded guests who keep asking, "Where should I sit?" Trying to work this out takes your eye off the ball, or should we say off the soup, and could cause a culinary disaster. Work it out beforehand and practice your calligraphy skills by writing place cards; even though it may seem a little old-fashioned, retro can be simply chic.

Tablecloth and Napkins

For fine dining, the tablecloth must be elegant. Personally, we find that less is more: a beautiful white tablecloth with touches of silver, taupe, gold, or bronze makes for a decadent backdrop.

Crisp napkins can be placed in beautiful napkin rings or neatly folded. If you can't do napkin origami, our advice is to go for a simple folded napkin placed on the plate.

Cutlery and Crockery

When laying your cutlery, it is good to take the butler approach, and if you don't happen to have a Mr. Carson from Downton Abbey available, here are some tips.

Place the service plate on the table directly in front of where your guest will be sitting.

The bread plate should be placed at the 10 o'clock position in relation to the dinner plate.

The butter knife should be placed on the bread plate in a diagonal position with the blade pointing up to eleven o' clock.

The dessert spoon is above the dinner plate, lying in a horizontal position, and the dessert fork lies above the dessert spoon in the opposite position.

All knives are placed on the right.

All forks are placed on the left.

The soup spoon is placed on the right. If soup is the first course, it will be placed the furthest away from the plate.

A water glass should be positioned at one o'clock in relation to the dinner plate, just above the knives.

The wine glass (red or white) should be placed to the right, below the water glass.

FESTIVE TABLES

Throughout the year we celebrate fantastic Jewish festivals. During these occasions, we are inclined to go a little more formal, but that doesn't mean our table has to look normal.

Passover Ideas

The Passover Seder table requires props to tell the Passover story. A beautiful Seder plate takes center stage and, of course, the matzo cover.

Since telling this epic story can take quite a while, the table can turn into part of the journey, especially if you have children who need to be occupied. We have amassed a collection of finger puppets depicting the plagues, wind-up matzo men who keep the little ones amused, and an amazing collection of *Hagaddahs* that are always a talking point, having been handed down from generation to generation. These hagaddahs keep everyone on their toes as the Passover story may be written slightly differently. It is wonderful to open a book where there is an inscription from a family member who may be joining us not at the table but looking down from up above.

Hagaddahs: Books used to tell the Passover story

Rosh Hashanah (The Jewish New Year) Ideas

For Rosh Hashanah, we cut pomegranates in half and core large apples, then place candles through the middle of the fruit and line them along the center of the table on small silver candle holders, creating a New Year to remember.

Honey can be used in many different ways—honey-scented candles or tiny honeypots that can be used for table name settings when labeled with a guest's name sticker on the front.

Table centerpieces can be created either by filling a glass bowl with bright green apples or taking a flowerpot, placing floral foam in the bottom, and attaching apples and pomegranates to wire spokes—there you have your own Rosh Hashanah masterpiece. You can also create these as gifts if you are lucky enough to be invited to someone else's table. If you really want to push the boat out, make a fantastic arrangement of assorted toffee apples dipped in sesame seeds, sprinkles, chocolate, etc. Edible table arrangements are a wonderful talking point and get everyone in the festive spirit. Don't panic: you have enough to cook, and these are available to purchase; we have checked!

Now that your table is set, it is time to set about cooking. And have we got some wonderful recipes for you!

OUR GADGET GIFT LIST

Call us impulsive, call us suckers, and call us a cab, because we can't fit the boxes into our trunk. Yes, Inspector Gadget, we are guilty as MasterCard, charged of purchasing yet another gizmo. It was the salesman that done it. We were innocently minding our own business when he accosted us in the frying pan department, with his slick hair, hypnotic eyes, and winning smile. We fell for his sincere *spiel*; we couldn't help ourselves, and he did look buff in that black apron. We believed his every syllable: "Hello, beautiful ladies." Our lives were about to be revolutionized. For that one day only, if we purchased two machines, we would get a third *free* (a brilliant Hanukkah gift)—a top-of-the-range, foodie fashionable, must-have giant juicer. (We were hanging onto three boxes like sumo wrestlers.)

These were the answers to our prayers. We would drink our way to glowing health; our hair would thicken and grow down to our waists; vitality would be our new middle name; our sisters-in-law would love their gifts and be forever in our debt. We would save a fortune on plastic surgery, turning back the hands of time, staying forever young, simply with fruit and vegetables. It was a win, win, *win*. What an investment. For only one hundred and fifty dollars, it was *cheap*! Plus, this unique juicer could do what no other juicer could do (besides making juice): it could separate skin and pith. There would be no more peeling, leaving only the vitamin-enriching, youth-enhancing elixir. Plus, it could de-shell and mill nuts faster than a team of squirrels. When the salesman gave us the demo, that was the clincher. He placed an unpeeled carrot in the machine, and the juice flowed. Wow, wow, wow, we said. Yes, yes, yes! And for that, we were also rewarded with a free thermos cup with its own handle. We were on a shopping high; it was the sale of the century!

Happily, the giant juicer did do what it said on the box, once we figured out how to open it and fit the jigsaw puzzle of pieces together (actually, the cleaner came to the rescue). We piled up my organic, exotic, eye-wateringly expensive fruits and vegetables. We couldn't wait to get going, and before you could say "blackberry, apple, lychee, mango, celery, and kale with a dash of ginger and lime," the juice flowed in double-quick time and a thimble full of nature's bounty stood before us. We knocked it back and felt totally re-energized. Finally, it was time for a wash. We began to dismantle the juicer to clean it (it took a while), and suddenly we realized our monumental, massive mistake after reading the words DO NOT PUT IN THE DISHWASHER printed on the side of the machine in large red letters. How could this have happened? The salesman hadn't told us that it wasn't dishwasher-proof; we don't *do* manual washing. An hour later of soaking, we were still picking lumps of pith, peel, and broken nails out of the machine!

We made a decision. The giant juicer and its two juicer friends (still in their boxes), together with the free cup, were on the move, back to the store.

We have all been found guilty of falling for a gizmo, as our kitchens and lofts are testament to. But occasionally we do track down an invaluable machine that does revolutionize our lives and save time, trouble, and shlepping. After much investigation here are six of the best:

Spiel: chat

THE KITCHENAID® or KENWOOD

This machine may seem like a huge investment, but it is best to go for the biggest and best model you can find. It will last you not only your lifetime but probably your children's. This mixer is the workhorse of the kitchen, whisking, beating, and dough-hooking you in. There are other more colorful mixers on the market, but the KitchenAid® or Kenwood are the strongest, quickest stallions. A food processor, e.g., a Magimix, may do the same job, but it doesn't hold nearly as much mixture, it isn't as easy to clean, and you have to figure out how to fit the processor's lid on without cracking the plastic (anyone else done that?).

HAND BLENDER/MINI CHOPPER

This really is a two-for-one deal. Make sure you invest in a high-powered model, as it will be smoothing out soup and chop, chop, chopping. A hand blender saves all the time and bother of decanting and pureeing soup into a liquidizer. Just make sure that when you are using the hand blender in any hot soup, hold it horizontal (avoiding the bottom of the pan) to miss out on a trip to the emergency room when hot soup splatters all over you.

As for the mini chopper, use it for chopping herbs, mixing dressings, and pulverizing nuts all in seconds; plus it makes you feel like a master chef.

POTATO RICER

What is a potato ricer, you may be wondering? A potato ricer is simple to use and easy to clean, and it creates a perfect mashed potato/sweet potato. Simply push cooked potato through the ricer—goodbye gloopy mash, hello restaurant-worthy pomme puree.

COFFEE MACHINE

The coffee machine has gone through a Nespresso revolution. Now you can be your own barista without studying at the bar. We are all turning into coffee addicts (and we have to control our addiction!). The coffee one drinks needs to be a full aroma moment. When these coffee machines launched, Hollywood-style, one couldn't help but be impressed by how handsome they were, how wonderful the coffee tasted, and how easy it was to froth milk. Now these super sleek machines have their own collection of coffee cups and capsules to match our kitchens. Advice: when choosing your machine, think about size and a style that works for you. As for the coffee, take time in-store to test which coffee you like. Just beware: if you drink too much, make sure you have plenty to do and plenty of money to spend as all that caffeine will transform you into a super speed-shopper who is shaking with excitement before she has even bought anything!

NUTRIBULLET (Or similar)

A Nutribullet or something similar really shakes it up. It whizzes fruit and vegetables in seconds. It is so simple to assemble anyone can do it, and best of all, it's dishwasher-proof. Here's a good tip: it also makes a wonderful chocolate malt Mars bar milkshake (we know that's not exactly what it was designed for, but sometimes a little of what you actually crave does you a world of good!).

HOT WATER TAP

The thought of having boiling hot water without flicking a switch and waiting for the kettle is the ultimate kitchen luxury. No de-scaling, really time-saving, more counter space on hand, and, to top it all, it looks great. The hot tap enables you to fill saucepans with boiling water to get your vegetables on the go and to make the gardener his morning brew before he can say, "Tea with eight sugars, please, and another slice of cake." This is the tap to tap into.

There are many other gizmos out there, but please, Inspector Gadget, can you invent a gadget that puts our gadgets together (including the plug) and explains how the things actually work?

SMALL PLATES

ASPARAGUS WITH HOLLANDAISE SAUCE

CHINESE CHICKEN SESAME TOAST

EGGPLANT GYOZA POT STICKERS

FALAFEL

JEWSHI JAPANESE GEFILTE FISH

MAGICAL MUSHROOMS

MINI EMPANADAS

MIDDLE EASTERN MEATBALLS

PRINCESS PITA (GREAT FOR PASSOVER)

STUFFED CONCHIGLIONI

Small plates give your guests a flavor of what's to come—a Premier Princess Production. They invite them to start conversing, discussing their favorite subject, *food*. Who needs a waitress? Before you know it, they will be helping themselves. Small plate service is particularly useful when you have guests who don't know each other well. As they pass around small, scrumptious plates of food, they will start sharing and caring about each other, and you never know, you might make a ***shidduch***.

Why go for a bowl of chips when you can offer a selection of dishes that even the most discerning guest cannot say no to? By creating an assortment of fabulous foods, you will have something to keep them going before they sit down to a menu of main courses, side dishes, desserts, and chocolates (in case they are still hungry).

When creating our small plates, we take inspiration from cultures around the world, turning to tapas, meze, and antipasti, serving up small dishes that still offer big tastes. Who says small can't be mighty?

Small plates don't need to be made just for dinner parties; they are multifunctional. A few dishes can be used for different occasions—lunches, girly get-togethers, canapé parties, baby blessings, etc. By simply replacing one hors d'oeuvre with a variety of small dishes, you instantly put the "party" into dinner party.

Just because something is small doesn't mean it isn't wonderful, a bit like us! We love fusion, mixing a little bit of this with a little bit of that (Prada and Chanel work beautifully together), and you never know what you can invent, even a new culinary term like *Jewshi*. Choose from chopped herring, egg, onion, or even gefilte fish, and wrap in rice and nori (seaweed) to create a sushi ***simcha*** special, a ***macher*** maki to impress your guests.

You just need a little imagination and some delicious ingredients. Don't worry about any extra work involved—these recipes are so quick, easy, and economical that your posh nosh will easily become part of your culinary repertoire, and your dinner parties will become the talk of the town.

Shidduch: Matching two people together, hopefully for marriage.
Simcha: Special occasion
Macher: Boss

ASPARAGUS WITH HOLLANDAISE SAUCE

SERVES 8

Don't be frightened, fellow Princesses, of this culinary classic—this hollandaise will amaze. You can make it prior to the event and slowly heat over a bain-marie when you wish to use.

Hollandaise is a marvelous accompaniment to poached salmon.

If you don't like asparagus and are looking for an alternative, roasted zucchini sticks are simply sensational.

Ingredients

Asparagus

Hollandaise Sauce
⅔ cup softened unsalted butter
4 medium egg yolks
2 tablespoons of lime juice
Rock salt

Method

Asparagus

For perfect asparagus, choose those that are in season. Trim the stalks, and for a restaurant look, peel the bottom of the asparagus a third of the way up.

Place in boiling, salted water and cover for 3–6 minutes.

To check that the asparagus is ready, i.e. al dente, place a fork in the stalk of one to make sure it is tender.

Drain. If not using straight away, place in an ice bath to keep its color. When cold, remove and dry with kitchen towels.

Season the asparagus with salt and black pepper.

Hollandaise Sauce

In a bain-marie (a heated saucepan of water with heatproof bowl resting on top that does not touch the water), melt the butter in the heatproof bowl until clarified. Turn down the heat.

In a separate bowl, whisk together egg yolks, lime juice, and salt until light and fluffy.

Keep the butter in the bain-marie so it stays warm, then slowly add it to the egg mixture, which is in a separate bowl, a ladle at a time. Keep whisking like your life depends upon it (this is a great arm workout). Each time a ladleful of the butter is absorbed into the egg mixture, add another until the butter has all been used up.

Place the hollandaise sauce back in the bain-marie. On very low heat, continue whisking until the mixture has thickened. This won't take very long, and suddenly you will have created the Princess Perfect Hollandaise.

Don't forget to season to taste.

CHINESE CHICKEN SESAME TOAST

MAKES 48 (IF MAKING TRIANGLES)

So sesame, so good, so *easy*.

Ingredients

9 oz minced chicken
1 large egg white
2 teaspoons soy sauce
¼ teaspoon garlic puree
½ teaspoon five-spice powder

Black pepper
6 slices white bread, crusts removed
1 tablespoon sesame seeds
Sweet chili sauce, to serve

Method

Mix chicken, egg white, soy sauce, garlic puree, five-spice powder, and black pepper to taste. Using a hand blender, blitz the ingredients to make a paste.

Take a slice of bread and spread the paste evenly over the top, edge to edge.

Scatter the sesame seeds on a plate. Turn the bread, paste side down, onto the seeds to get an even coating.

With a sharp knife, cut into squares, triangles, slices, or however you like.

Heat oil in a frying pan. When hot, cook the slices for approximately 3 minutes, turning halfway through cooking, until golden brown on both sides. Place on kitchen towel to remove excess oil.

Serve with sweet chili sauce on the side.

EGGPLANT GYOZA POT STICKERS

MAKES 18

The Japanese alternative to **kreplach**. Delicious when dipped into sweet chili sauce.

Kreplach: Jewish ravioli

Ingredients

1 large eggplant, skin removed and diced finely
2 tablespoons olive oil, for frying eggplant
Salt
Black Pepper

2 teaspoons mirin
18 wheat dumpling wrappers
1 tablespoon olive oil, for coating frying pan

Method

Fry the eggplant in olive oil until brown. Season with salt and pepper. Place in a bowl and stir in mirin.

Place a teaspoon of eggplant in the middle of a wrapper. Fold the pastry into a half moon shape and stick the edges together with water. With your forefinger and thumb, pinch the outside of the pastry along the rim.

Coat a frying pan with olive oil and heat. Place the gyoza pot stickers with the flat edge on the pan. Fry and turn until both sides are brown.

Take a couple of tablespoons of water and sprinkle over the gyoza pot stickers. Quickly place a lid on the frying pan, and allow to steam for a couple of minutes until the pot stickers have puffed up.

FALAFEL

MAKES APPROXIMATELY 55 MINI BALLS

Every Princess should try this recipe. There is nothing like eating these homemade unless you are on Dizengoff Street in Tel Aviv.

Ingredients

5½ cups drained, canned chickpeas, rinsed
1 large onion, diced
1 tablespoon garlic puree
1 teaspoon ground cilantro
1 teaspoon turmeric
1 teaspoon ginger puree
1 oz flat leaf parsley, chopped
1 tablespoon cilantro, chopped
¼ cup toasted pine nuts (toast in a dry frying pan)

1⅓ cup self-rising flour
2 tablespoons olive oil
1 lemon rind grated
½ lemon juice
Salt
Black pepper
Vegetable oil, for frying
1 cup self-rising flour (leveled), for rolling

Method

In a food processor, mix together all the ingredients except the vegetable oil and self-rising flour. You will need plenty of salt, so check the seasoning. Blend the ingredients until you achieve a coarse consistency

Heat vegetable oil in a shallow frying pan. Grab a teaspoon of mixture and form a ball with damp hands. Roll in the flour and fry in hot oil until golden on each side, approximately 7–10 minutes in total.

Lay on kitchen paper to remove any excess oil.

JEWSHI JAPANESE GEFILTE FISH

SERVES 4 AS A STARTER OR 12 AS CANAPÉS

Gefilte fusion is a *great* new specialty Jewshi dish.

Ingredients

Gefilte Fish

1 lb minced white fish (a mix of haddock, whiting, and bream; you can get this from your fishmonger)

1 large onion, grated

1 large carrot, grated

½ cup fine matzo meal

2 medium eggs

1 tablespoon superfine sugar

1 teaspoon table salt

Black pepper

1 teaspoon dried parsley

Toppings

Chrain (horseradish with beet, available in kosher delicatessens or online)

1 tablespoon toasted sesame seeds (pan-fry dry, and they will soon turn golden)

Japanese ginger (available in Japanese supermarkets)

Method

Mix all ingredients for the gefilte fish in a large bowl and leave for a few minutes to set.

Take a large piece of cling wrap (check that it's safe for cooking with) and place the gefilte fish mix on top. Roll the gefilte fish into a long, even sausage shape and wrap up with the cling wrap, twisting the edges so the fish is completely sealed.

Place the gefilte fish in a large shallow saucepan filled with water. Bring to boil, then simmer for 20 minutes with the lid on.

Remove from the water and leave to cool. Refrigerate.

When ready to serve, remove the cling wrap and cut into 12 even pieces (we use an electric carving knife). Place each piece on a serving plate. Add a teaspoon of chrain in the center.

Sprinkle sesame seeds over the fish and garnish with ginger.

MAGICAL MUSHROOMS

MAKES 8

Stuffed mushrooms are simply sensational.

Ingredients

8 large flat chestnut mushrooms
⅔ cup of full-fat cream cheese
4 tablespoons of crème fraîche
1 red chili finely diced
½ teaspoon garlic puree
1 handful flat leaf parsley, chopped
1 handful fresh basil, chopped

Salt
Black pepper
3 slices of bread, made into breadcrumbs (Put day-old bread of choice in a blender and chop to make breadcrumbs; you can also buy ready-made)
1½ cups grated mozzarella

Method

Preheat oven to 350°F / 180°C.

Wrap each mushroom in silver foil. Bake for 30 minutes. Remove from foil, draining any excess liquid.

Mix together all other ingredients except breadcrumbs and mozzarella, seasoning with salt and black pepper, to make a cream cheese mixture.

In a separate bowl, mix together breadcrumbs and mozzarella.

Fill each mushroom with the cream cheese mixture. Top with the breadcrumb mixture and a little extra salt and black pepper.

Bake for 10–15 minutes until golden brown.

MINI EMPANADAS
MAKES APPROXIMATELY 35

If you don't want to use all of these delicious pastries at once, leave a batch uncooked and open freeze them (this means freezing uncovered; once the empanadas are frozen, you can cover or place in a plastic box in the freezer). When you have guests over, simply take them straight from the freezer and heat them in the oven for approximately 30 minutes or until golden brown. For a vegetarian option, just leave out the kabanos.

Ingredients

4 tablespoons olive oil
1 sweet potato, peeled and finely diced
1 clove garlic, crushed
1 onion, diced
1 small eggplant, finely diced and sliced
3 mini kabanos, finely diced
1 small yellow bell pepper, finely diced
½ teaspoon sweet paprika

1 tablespoon balsamic vinegar
Salt
Black pepper
2 puff pastry sheets (1½ lb total)
Flour, to dust
Cookie cutter, approximately 3 inches in diameter
2 large eggs, lightly whisked

Method

Heat olive oil in a pan. Fry the sweet potato. Add the crushed garlic. When the sweet potato begins to soften, add the onions, eggplant, kabanos, and bell pepper. Heat olive oil in a pan. Fry the sweet potato. Add the crushed garlic.

Add the paprika, balsamic vinegar, salt, and pepper. Continue to stir until all the vegetables soften. Transfer the ingredients to another dish and leave to cool.

Preheat the oven to 350°F / 180°C.

Lay out the pastry sheet on a floured board and cut out circles with your cookie cutter. Roll any leftover pastry out again, and cut. In total, you should make approximately 18 empanadas from one sheet of pastry. Repeat the whole process with the second sheet.

Brush the perimeter of each pastry circle with egg wash. In the center of each pastry, place a heaped teaspoon of the vegetable mixture. Take one side of the pastry and close over the mixture to form a half crescent, pressing the edges down and crimping with your fingers.

Line a baking tray with parchment paper. Place the mini empanadas on the baking tray, then dip a pastry brush into the whisked egg and spread over the top of the empanadas. This gives them a beautiful shine.

Bake for approximately 20–25 minutes until the pastry is golden brown.

MIDDLE EASTERN MEATBALLS

MAKES APPROXIMATELY 40

Serve in warm pita with fried onions and humus, you will be transported to the old city of Jerusalem—you wouldn't even need a magic carpet.

Ingredients

1½ lb lean beef, minced
1 large egg
1 teaspoon dried parsley
1 teaspoon dried turmeric
1 teaspoon dried cumin
1 teaspoon dried cilantro

1 teaspoon sumac
½ teaspoon garlic puree paste
Grated lemon rind
1 tablespoon medium matzo meal
Salt
Black pepper

Method

Mix all the ingredients in a large bowl.

Take a teaspoon of mixture and, with wet hands, shape into a small ball. Place on a flat-rimmed tray lined with baking parchment. Open freeze (uncovered) for a minimum of 30 minutes.

Once frozen, place in an airtight container and put back in the freezer, covered, until ready to use, or remove and place on a lined baking tray and bake in a preheated oven at 350°F / 180°C for approximately 15–20 minutes until cooked all the way through.

PRINCESS PITA
(GREAT FOR PASSOVER)

MAKES 12

Perfect for those Passover lunches—layer up with smoked salmon, egg salad or a variety of different toppings. Just use your imagination, and think of this is your own pita bar. It can be eaten hot or cold, and store in the refrigerator.

Ingredients

½ lb boiled mashed potatoes (approximately 3 potatoes suitable for mashing; use a potato ricer)

1 teaspoon dried parsley

2 large eggs

1⅓ cups medium matzo meal

Salt

Black pepper

2 tablespoons potato flour

Vegetable oil, for frying

Method

Leave the mashed potatoes until they are completely cool, before use.

Add the parsley, eggs, and matzo meal to the mashed potatoes and mix together. Season with salt and pepper to taste.

Cover your hands with potato flour. Take a tablespoon of the mixture and, using your hands, pat until flat to resemble a small pita bread.

Pour a thin layer of oil in a frying pan. Fry in the oil until golden on each side, turning halfway through. Place on kitchen towels to remove any excess grease.

STUFFED CONCHIGLIONI

SERVES 8

A great dish that can easily be made ahead of time. If doing so, just refrigerate the conchiglioni after you have stuffed the shells, and when ready to use heat for 15 minutes in a hot oven. Serve the conchiglioni preferably with a red serviette to follow the Italian theme and to stop you staining your new Italian Dolce & Gabana dress.

Ingredients

8½ oz conchiglioni (20 large pasta shells dried)
1 tablespoon olive oil, for cooking the pasta
4 tablespoons olive oil, for frying (plus extra to drizzle)
2 sweet shallots, finely diced
1 eggplant, finely diced

1 teaspoon of dried oregano
Salt
Black pepper
2 oz small tomatoes, diced
1 cup mozzarella, diced into small pieces
8 fresh basil leaves

Method

Preheat oven to 350°F / 180°C.

Place the conchiglioni in a saucepan of salted boiling water with 1 tablespoon olive oil, and cook for approximately 15 minutes until al dente. You need 16 perfect shells, but cook 20 in case any split. Drain and leave to one side.

Heat olive oil in a large frying pan, add the diced shallots, and sweat.

Add eggplant and oregano, season with salt and black pepper, and fry until soft.

Take off the heat and mix in the diced tomatoes.

Take a tablespoon of the mixture and place in each shell, along with a few pieces of diced mozzarella. In an oven-proof dish, top each shell with half a basil leaf. Drizzle with more olive oil, and season with salt and black pepper.

Bake in the oven for approximately 15 minutes.

SENSATIONAL SOUP

ASPARAGUS & CAULIFLOWER VISCHYSSOISE

CANNELLINI BEAN TOMATO SOUP

LENTIL SOUP

QUINOA VEGETABLE MINESTRONE

RED CABBAGE, BEET & APPLE BORSCHT

SEPHARDI SAFFRON CHICKEN SOUP WITH FRAGRANT MATZO BALLS

SWEETCORN CHOWDER

VIETNAMESE VEGETARIAN PHO SOUP

YEMENITE MEAT SOUP

WATERCRESS SOUP

There are many areas of cooking that can be technically challenging, and for some, it's just stepping through the kitchen door. Rather like the thought of going to the gym, it's not always on the top of one's to-do list. But we assure you, once you get in there and the work is done, you will be filled with a wonderful sense of satisfaction—and you'll simply love the results. However, just like working out, there is no point starting out by running the marathon, as you won't get very far. What you need is some training to understand the fundamentals.

Soup is an ideal starting point—not only can it be served as the start to a meal, it can make a lovely lunch or a meal in a mug; it's quick to make and economical on your Princess Pocket; and if you make too much, most soups freeze fabulously. Unlike a pastry that doesn't puff, a custard that curdles, or a sauce that splits, *it is very rare* to sink a soup.

It is all about fresh ingredients, herbs, and spices, and the only tools you will need are a sharp knife, a chopping board, a saucepan, and a great blender (have you tried a Vitamix®?).

Soup, like your wardrobe, changes with the season. You wouldn't consider wearing heavy combat boots to go for a long walk on a hot summer's day, just as you wouldn't make a thick lentil soup to **shvitz** on a hot summer's night. However, for us, there is one exception to this golden rule: the iconic Jewish Princess chicken soup, which our family enjoys all year round. We have even given this chicken soup recipe a summer shake-up, our delicious Sephardi Saffron Chicken Soup with Fragrant Matzo Balls (page 47). It is full of flavor, color, and can be made express style by using just chicken wings.

Soups are packed with vitamins and minerals, many of them giving you part of your five a day—perfect for Princess Gym Bunnies. For hot green juice, see our Watercress Soup (page 53), full of vitamins and minerals. In the winter, what better way to fuel your body than with a wholesome, flavorsome soup filled with fresh and seasonal ingredients like Yemenite Meat Soup (page 52) or the fashionable Quinoa Vegetable Minestrone, (page 43), especially if you do happen to be training for the marathon, shopping, or otherwise? In the summer months, try a chilled Asparagus & Cauliflower Vichyssoise (page 40) to cool you down after a terrific tennis match or yoga on your own private beach on your own private island (we have the brochure). This recipe makes a super starter or a lovely light lunch.

Soup is not only simple to cook—with a few extra ingredients you can soup it up and transform it into a meal in a bowl. Try adding pasta (whole wheat for those Health Nuts) or, our personal favorite, short twists of strozzapreti pasta. How about rice, quinoa or couscous, or croutons (a great way to use up stale bread)? And what Jewish family could get by without that vital tub of Osem's yellow mini croutons? Friday just wouldn't be Friday without them. For dairy soups, grated cheese may be a little naughty, but it is also very nice. To top it off, add a swirl of cream or crème fraîche (you can buy half-fat); after all, with all that working out, you deserve it.

To buy a ready-made soup in our opinion is soup sacrilege; they are usually filled with additives and preservatives and have an unsatisfactory after-taste that gives soup a bad name (yuck). As for soup that comes in a packet, by the time you have read all the ingredients on the back of the package, you could have whipped up a tasty broth with all your leftover vegetables. We are not even going to mention canned soup, because with our simple recipes, creating a delicious homemade soup will be a walk in the park—it *can* be something you *can* do.

Shvitz: Sweat

ASPARAGUS & CAULIFLOWER VICHYSSOISE

SERVES 4–6

Serve with a swirl of cream and fresh dill for extra decadence.

Ingredients

1 large onion, diced
1 leek, diced
3 pints vegetable stock (made with 1½ tablespoons vegetable bouillon powder)
1½ cups peeled chopped potatoes
2 celery sticks, chopped
1 tablespoon dried parsley

Salt
Black pepper
8 oz asparagus, chopped
12 oz cauliflower, chopped
2 fl oz full-fat milk
¼ whole nutmeg, grated (or ¼ teaspoon nutmeg powder)

Method

In a saucepan, heat the olive oil. Sweat onion and leek.

Add the vegetable stock, potatoes, celery, and parsley. Season with salt and black pepper. Bring to a boil, then simmer for 20 minutes.

Add the asparagus and cauliflower. Simmer for a further 20 minutes.

Add the rest of the ingredients and blend with a hand blender until smooth. Check seasoning—if you wish to add a little more nutmeg, be my guest.

Once cool, refrigerate and then eat cold (but it does taste great hot as well).

CANNELLINI BEAN TOMATO SOUP

SERVES 8

An Italian stallion of a soup.

Ingredients

2 tablespoons olive oil
3 medium onions, diced
2 large carrots, peeled and diced
3 large zucchini, diced
1 lb drained canned cannellini beans (rinsed)
2¼ lb tomato passata (a specific type of ready-
    made tomato puree that is not cooked and
    has had the skins and seeds removed; sieved
    tomatoes)

1 teaspoon dried sage
1 teaspoon dried or fresh rosemary
2 tablespoons superfine sugar
2½ pints vegetable stock (made with
    2 tablespoons vegetable bouillon powder)
Salt
Black Pepper

Method

In a deep saucepan, heat the olive oil. Sweat the onions in olive oil until translucent.

Add the carrots, zucchini, beans, tomato passata, sage, rosemary, sugar, and bouillon powder.
Season with salt and black pepper.

Bring to a boil and leave to simmer until the vegetables are soft. This will take approximately 45
minutes.

Blend the soup until smooth. If it's too thick for your taste, add a little water. Check seasoning.

LENTIL SOUP

SERVES 6–8

A modern vegetarian alternative to bean and barley soup—so good.

Ingredients

2 tablespoons olive oil

2 large onions, finely chopped

2 leeks, finely chopped

16 oz pre-soaked lentils (cover with water, leave overnight, and rinse well; or use canned)

2 potatoes, diced

3 large carrots, diced

2 bay leaves, torn

1 tablespoon dried parsley

3 pints vegetable stock (made with 2 tablespoons vegetable bouillon powder)

Salt

Black pepper

Method

In a large saucepan, heat the oil. Sweat onions and leeks in oil.

Add the rest of the ingredients and bring to a boil. Simmer for approximately 30 minutes or until vegetables and lentils are soft. Check seasoning.

QUINOA VEGETABLE MINESTRONE

SERVES 6–8

An unusual take on this Italian classic, a bit like Dolce & Gabana meets Brioni. Try to cut all the vegetables to a similar size.

Ingredients

2 tablespoons olive oil
1 large onion, finely diced
2 leeks, diced
1 butternut squash, diced
1 large zucchini, diced
4 oz green beans, chopped
1 heart celery stick, thinly sliced
1 teaspoon garlic puree
1 teaspoon superfine sugar

Water, enough to cover the vegetables
4 oz red and white quinoa
1 tablespoon vegetable bouillon powder (we like Marigold)
1 teaspoon dried rosemary
2 bay leaves, torn
Salt
Pepper

Method

Heat olive oil in a deep saucepan. Fry onions and leeks until slightly translucent.

Add the rest of the vegetables, garlic puree, and sugar.

Boil the water, and pour to cover vegetables. Add quinoa and bouillon powder. Add on the remaining herbs, and season with salt and pepper.

Bring to a boil, and then simmer for approximately 25–30 minutes with the lid on until the vegetables are soft.

RED CABBAGE, BEET & APPLE BORSCHT

SERVES 6–8

A sweet and sour summer soup, a bit like the British weather!

Ingredients

1 large onion, diced
1 teaspoon olive oil
3 pink lady apples (6 oz), peeled and cut into
    quarters
1 lb red cabbage, shredded and diced
4 large beets (14 oz), peeled and cubed
4 tablespoons apple cider vinegar

2 tablespoons superfine sugar
2 tablespoons vegetable bouillon dissolved in
    2½ pints water
Salt
Good dollop of sour cream per person
    (non-dairy alternative: a good squeeze of
    lemon)

Method

In a large saucepan, sweat the onion in the olive oil.

Add the apple, cabbage, beet, apple cider vinegar, superfine sugar, and vegetable stock, and salt to season.

Bring to a boil and simmer for approximately 40 minutes. Liquidize well and check seasoning.

Serve hot or cold with a good dollop of sour cream or, if not using dairy, a good squeeze of lemon juice.

SEPHARDI SAFFRON CHICKEN SOUP WITH FRAGRANT MATZO BALLS

SERVES 6

A fragrant bowl of **kneidlach**—Jewish Penicillin.

Kneidlach: Dumplings

Ingredients

Sephardi Soup

8 large chicken wings
8 pints cold water
2 large carrots, peeled
2 large celery sticks, trimmed
1 parsnip, peeled
1 turnip, peeled
1 large white onion, peeled

1 rutabaga, peeled
2 bay leaves, torn
1 small bunch cilantro
3 chicken bouillon cubes
Salt
Pepper
1 pinch saffron melted in 1 fl oz boiled water

Method

Sephardi Soup

Place the wings in a large saucepan. Pour in the water and bring to a boil. With a large spoon, skim off the scum from the top.

Add the rest of the ingredients except the saffron. Bring the soup back to a boil and simmer for 2 hours with the lid on.

Remove from heat and discard all the vegetables, but keep the chicken wings to one side. Place back in the soup once the vegetables have been removed. Add the saffron to the chicken broth.

Leave to cool and refrigerate overnight.

When ready to use, remove the fat from the top of the soup (you can do this with a spoon or by laying a wad of kitchen paper over the top and removing it).

Ingredients

Fragrant Matzo Balls (makes approximately 24)
¾ cup medium matzo meal
¾ cup ground almonds
3 large eggs, lightly whisked
2 tablespoons olive oil
1 teaspoon table salt

½ teaspoon baking powder
1 teaspoon ground ginger
1 tablespoon lemon juice
½ lemon rind, zested
1 small bunch cilantro, stalks removed and finely chopped (reserve 1 tablespoon to serve)

Method

Fragrant Matzo Balls

Mix all the ingredients to form the mixture, but reserve 1 tablespoon of cilantro. Place the mixture in the fridge for approximately 20 minutes.

Remove from the fridge. Wet your hands, take a teaspoon of mixture, and roll into a ball. Carry on doing this with the rest of the mixture.

Fill a medium sized saucepan with boiling salted water. Transfer the matzo balls into the boiling water and continue cooking on a strong simmer for 20 minutes, turning occasionally.

Remove balls with a slotted spoon and leave to cool.

When ready to serve, heat the soup slowly with the matzo balls until piping hot. Serve 4 matzo balls per person and a sprinkle of chopped cilantro.

SWEETCORN CHOWDER

SERVES 6

If you'd like to, add some cooked shredded chicken when serving. Go ahead, amigo!

Ingredients

1 large onion, chopped
2 tablespoons olive oil
3 pints chicken or vegetable stock (made with 1½ tablespoons stock powder)
18 oz whole kernel sweet corn, frozen

1 red chili, chopped and de-seeded
1 tablespoon flat leaf parsley, chopped
1 red bell pepper, chopped
4 scallions, chopped
½ bunch fresh cilantro, chopped

Method

Sweat the chopped onion in olive oil.

Add the vegetable stock, whole kernel sweet corn, chili, and parsley. Bring to a boil and simmer for approximately 20 minutes until the corn is soft.

Blend using a hand blender.

In a separate saucepan, add the chopped red pepper to water (approximately 7 fl oz). Bring to a boil and simmer for approximately 15 minutes. Remove pepper from the water with a slotted spoon.

Add the red pepper, chopped scallions, and chopped cilantro to the soup. Serve.

VIETNAMESE VEGETARIAN PHO SOUP

SERVES 4

A veggie feast of a soup; the world's your oyster mushroom!

Ingredients

Vegetable Broth

1 star anise
4 cloves
½ teaspoon ground cilantro
1 red onion, chopped
1 large carrot, chopped
2 celery sticks, chopped
3 pints vegetable stock (made with 1½ tablespoons vegetable bouillon)
½ teaspoon garlic puree
1 teaspoon soy sauce
1 teaspoon hoisin sauce
Black pepper

Toppings (Your Choice)

1 red chili, finely diced
4 scallions, chopped
1 red onion, finely sliced
1 oz ginger, grated
4 oz cooked rice noodles (follow instructions on packet)
Selection of steamed vegetables (mushrooms, bok choy, asparagus, carrots, sugar snap peas, etc.)
5 oz tofu, chopped
1 oz fresh cilantro, chopped
2 soft hard-boiled eggs
1 lime, cut into fine wedges

Method

Dry fry all anise, cloves, and cilantro until smoking. Turn off the heat.

Add the rest of the broth ingredients. Bring to a boil, then simmer on low heat for 15 minutes, remove from heat, and pour through a sieve.

Place broth in the center of the table and your selection of toppings all around for guests to pick and choose. It is better to serve the vegetables straight from the steamer.

YEMENITE MEAT SOUP

SERVES 6–8

A Middle Eastern soup that will spice up your life. For extra spice, add a small teaspoon of zhug (available at Middle Eastern grocery stores) to each bowl. Make this soup a day before to allow the flavors to enhance.

Ingredients

1½ lb chuck steak, cubed

7 pints water

2 tablespoons Hawaij (a spice mix available at Middle Eastern grocery stores)

1 teaspoon salt

2 tablespoons beef stock powder (or 1 cube)

1 clove garlic

2 lb pumpkin, chopped

2 lb potatoes, chopped

5 fresh large tomatoes, chopped

2 large onions, chopped

1 bunch scallions

2 tablespoons cilantro leaves, chopped

Method

Cover the cubed chuck steak with water and bring to a boil. Leave to simmer, removing any scum.

When the water is clear, add the rest of the ingredients and simmer for approximately 4 hours until the meat is soft—do not cover.

WATERCRESS SOUP

SERVES 6

If you wish, add a swirl of cream. Watercress is simply wonderful. It is high in calcium—fabulous for your Princess Pearly whites.

Ingredients

1 large onion, diced
1 large leek, diced
1 tablespoon olive oil
1 large potato, peeled and chopped
6 celery sticks, diced

3 pints vegetable stock (made with 1 tablespoon bouillon mixed with hot water)
10 oz watercress (remove the thick parts of the stalk)
Salt
Black pepper

Method

In a large saucepan, sweat the onion and leek in olive oil until translucent.

Add potato, celery, and vegetable stock. Bring to a boil and simmer for 30 minutes with the saucepan lid on.

Add the watercress and continue cooking for 4 minutes.

Remove from heat and blend using a hand blender.

Season with salt and black pepper.

SALADS—GO GREEN

ADZUKI, WASABI & BELL PEPPER SALAD

BEJEWELED SWEET POTATO, BEET & POMEGRANATE SALAD

BRIE PEAR & CARAMELIZED WALNUTS ON ENDIVE LEAVES

CARROT, COCONUT & GINGER SALAD

HORSERADISH NEW POTATO SALAD

ROASTED CELERY ROOT SALAD

ROASTED RED BELL PEPPER & TUNA SALAD WITH SHERRY VINEGAR

SHARON PERSIMMON FRUIT & SUGAR SNAP PEA SALAD

WARM JERUSALEM SALAD

TOMATO GAZPACHO SALAD

Salads have undergone a revolution. The days of limp lettuce, a few slices of cucumber, a sad tomato, and a dollop of salad dressing are no more. Calorific, greasy, store-bought coleslaw—with that awful, tangy, vinegary taste—has been assigned to the annals of history.

The trend to go green has made us look into our own backyards to find delicious ingredients to fill our salad bowls. We all want a taste of the good life, even if it is just a matter of planting a few pots with wonderful herbs, or going for **the whole megillah** and investing in a greenhouse and a sexy gardener (We hear the one from *Desperate Housewives* is looking for a job). If that isn't adventurous enough, one can always look further afield and try out the latest craze: foraging (not for a gardener, but for food; and not for chocolate truffles, but for real truffles!). However, we must admit that we haven't gone down to the woods to trudge through mud; a Princess must think of her nails. We simply go to the supermarket and search the shelves, which are filled with a wonderful array of enticing vegetables, all organic and still growing (have you seen the lettuce that is sold in its own grow box?), ready sliced and diced for the lazy cooks among us (that would be us!). Then there are dwarfed species—mini zucchinis, bell peppers, and eggplants. And how about finishing your bowl with a few edible flowers to really give your salad that special bouquet? If you don't like a bowl of salad, how about a "glass of salad"? After all, juicers are now more popular than Juicy Couture.

It's not only the vegetables that make salads a truly superfood dish, it is also the limitless array of other ingredients that can be added to give taste, texture, and, of course, crunch. Nuts, seeds, fruit, herbs, spices, and even a few carbs thrown in that will not make your Jewish Princess dinner guests run for the hills. The fact is, girls, that we do *need* our carbs; just try and make them like you—*complex*!

When creating a salad you can take your inspiration from every nation—a Spanish Tomato Gazpacho Salad (page 70) or Japanese Adzuki, Wasabi & Bell Pepper Salad (page 58), or the French Brie Pear & Caramelized Walnuts on Endive Leaves (page 61).

To finish a salad, one must indulge in a little designer dressing, never a Princess Problem. Use your ingredients wisely—flavored oils, citrus for zing, yogurt, spices, seasoning, herbs . . . The list is endless, but the aim is always the same—to create balance and harmony, yin and yang. It's all a matter of good taste, and we Princesses know all about that. Chop, crush, and mix your ingredients well, give your dressing a good shake before pouring, and *never* dress too early, as your salad will *not* make an entrance but rather a swift exit. Invest in a mini-processor; they really are fantastic if chopping isn't your thing, and they make the whole process so quick and easy.

When serving a salad, pile high on a plate or use a giant salad bowl, and if going for the layered look, use glass so that your salad can be viewed from every angle. A salad is a gastronomic work of art, nature at its best. The salads we have created for you in this chapter are not just a bit on the side; they are a masterpiece, your very own Princess Picasso.

The whole megillah: The whole thing

ADZUKI, WASABI & BELL PEPPER SALAD

SERVES 6–8

A tasty, refreshing, mean bean salad full of fiber and minerals.

Ingredients

2 red bell peppers, sliced and de-seeded
Olive oil spray
13 oz fine green beans, topped and tailed
3 celery sticks, thinly sliced
14-oz can Adzuki beans, thoroughly rinsed (8 oz when drained)

Dressing
1 teaspoon garlic paste
1½ teaspoons wasabi paste
4 tablespoons olive oil
1 lemon, juiced
2 tablespoons dark brown sugar
Salt
Back pepper

Method

Preheat oven to 350°F / 180°C.

Place the peppers in an ovenproof dish. Spray with olive oil, and place in the oven to roast for 30 minutes.

In a saucepan filled with salted boiling water, place the green beans and boil until al dente. Drain and rinse with cold water, and then chop in half.

In a serving bowl, put the celery, adzuki beans, green beans, and roasted red pepper slices.

Mix all the ingredients for the dressing, and pour over the salad, mixing thoroughly.

BEJEWELED SWEET POTATO, BEET & POMEGRANATE SALAD

SERVES 6–8

A feast of colors creates a jewel of a dish.

For meals when you don't wish to use dairy products in your salad, just drizzle over a little framboise vinegar and fresh lemon juice, omitting the crème fraîche.

Ingredients

3 beets
6 sweet potatoes, peeled and cut into large chunks
1 tablespoon olive oil
Rock salt

Black pepper
3½ fl oz half-fat crème fraîche
½ lemon, juiced
1 pomegranate, reserve seeds
Fresh cilantro, chopped

Method

Preheat oven to 375°F / 190°C.

Wrap each beet in silver foil. Toss sweet potatoes in olive oil. Bake beets and sweet potatoes in the oven until soft, approximately 60 minutes. Remove and leave to cool—unwrap the beets from their foil.

When the beets are cool, the skin will come off easily in your hands (it is advisable to use plastic gloves to prevent staining). Cut the beets into large chunks.

Place the sweet potatoes and beets on a serving plate. Season with salt and black pepper.

In a separate bowl, mix crème fraîche and lemon juice. Blob the crème fraîche mixture over the salad.

Sprinkle with pomegranate seeds and chopped cilantro. Check seasoning; add a little more salt and black pepper if necessary.

BRIE PEAR & CARAMELIZED WALNUTS ON ENDIVE LEAVES

SERVES 8

Walnuts are great for the brain, but this dish is so easy it simply is a no-brainer.

Ingredients

1 tablespoon unsalted butter
2 tablespoons brown sugar
1½ cups walnuts
4 red pears, sliced
1 teaspoon vanilla essence
8 oz Brie cheese, chopped
5 oz red endive leaves
Black pepper

Dressing
1 tablespoon apple cider vinegar
½ tablespoon white wine vinegar
2½ tablespoons extra virgin olive oil
½ teaspoon garlic puree
2 teaspoons superfine sugar
Salt
Black pepper

Method

In a small frying pan, melt the butter. Add the brown sugar and walnuts. Toss, coating the walnuts with butter and sugar. Fry the walnuts until caramelized and leave to one side.

Place sliced pears in a saucepan and add boiling water, enough to cover the pears. Add vanilla essence. Cook for approximately 2 minutes or until the pears are slightly soft. Remove from water and leave to cool.

Mix nuts, pears, and Brie together with endive leaves. Arrange like a work of art, and season with black pepper.

Mix all ingredients for the dressing together, and dress your salad just before serving.

CARROT, COCONUT & GINGER SALAD

SERVES 4–6

The Eastern flavors give this salad a delicious aroma—and it doesn't taste too bad, either.

Ingredients

2¼ lb Chantenay carrots, peeled
Salt
Black pepper
2 teaspoons freshly grated ginger

2 teaspoons freshly grated coconut (or desiccated)
2 teaspoons light soy sauce
2 teaspoons clear honey
1 teaspoon lemon juice

Method

Cook carrots in boiling water until al dente, approximately 10 minutes. Strain and place in iced water. Drain again and place in a serving bowl. Season with salt and pepper to taste.

Add the rest of the ingredients. Toss the carrots well.

HORSERADISH NEW POTATO SALAD

SERVES 6

This delicious salad can be served warm or cold, and is the perfect accompaniment to cold meat.

Ingredients

2¼ lb baby new potatoes
2 oz black olives, pitted
3 oz chargrilled artichokes, chopped (buy ready-made)
1 oz sundried tomatoes in sunflower oil, chopped

Good glug of oil from artichokes or sundried tomatoes
1 heaped tablespoon creamed horseradish
Black pepper

Method

Place potatoes in a saucepan filled with water to cover. Bring to a boil and simmer until you can easily cut through a potato, approximately 15 minutes.

Remove from heat and drain. Cut the potatoes in half.

Add the rest of the ingredients while the potatoes are still warm, making sure everything is well incorporated.

ROASTED CELERY ROOT SALAD

SERVES 6–8

Though less fattening than a potato, this salad gives you that "carb" sense of satisfaction.

Ingredients

2 large celery roots, peeled and cut into thick
   wedges

2 tablespoons olive oil

1 teaspoon dried sage

Salt

Black pepper

½ lemon, juiced

1 lemon, zested

1 lime, zested

Method

Preheat oven to 350°F / 180°C.

Place the celery root on a lined baking sheet. Coat with 1 tablespoon of olive oil (reserve the second tablespoon for the dressing) and sprinkle with sage. Season to taste with salt and pepper.

Bake for approximately 45 minutes. Remove from oven and dice the celery root.

Dress with a good squeeze of fresh lemon juice and 1 tablespoon of olive oil, and sprinkle with lemon and lime zest. Check seasoning.

ROASTED RED BELL PEPPER & TUNA SALAD WITH SHERRY VINEGAR

SERVES 4

This is a great lunch dish; it takes me straight to the Spanish beaches (yes, please). As a canapé, take a tablespoon of mixture and place on a pretty serving spoon, and offer on a tray to your guest.

Ingredients

2 medium red bell peppers, sliced thinly
1 jar (8 oz) Albacore tuna in extra virgin oil, flaked
Rock salt
½ red onion, finely diced
7 scallions, finely chopped (use only the white end)

½ black Spanish pitted olives, sliced
¾ cup canned red kidney beans
2 dessert spoons sherry vinegar
1 small bunch flat-leaf parsley, chopped
Salt
Black pepper

Method

Preheat oven to 400°F / 200°C.

Cover the bell peppers in the oil from the tuna, and season with rock salt.

Oven roast the bell peppers in an oven-proof dish for approximately 40 minutes until soft. Remove and leave to cool.

In a mixing bowl, place the drained flaked tuna. Add the red onion, scallions, and olives.

Drain and thoroughly wash kidney beans, dry with kitchen towels, and incorporate into the salad.

When the red peppers have cooled, mix with the sherry vinegar and toss into the salad.

Add the chopped parsley. Season with salt and black pepper.

SHARON PERSIMMON FRUIT & SUGAR SNAP PEA SALAD

SERVES 6–8

The trick to this refreshing salad is to chop all the ingredients to a similar size.

Ingredients

2 large persimmons
16 oz sugar snap peas, sliced
1 pink grapefruit
3 large avocados, diced
6 mint leaves, finely sliced

1 tablespoon fresh cilantro, chopped
1 tablespoon olive oil
½ lemon, juiced
Salt

Method

Remove the stalk of the persimmon, and then dice or thinly slice (we leave it to you). Add sugar snap peas to the persimmon.

Peel and remove the pith of the grapefruit and chop into small segments. Add grapefruit and avocados.

Add mint leaves and cilantro.

Drizzle the olive oil and lemon juice over the ingredients. Sprinkle with salt.

Toss the salad gently and serve immediately.

WARM JERUSALEM SALAD

SERVES 4

A little bit of Eretz Israel in your kitchen.

Ingredients

1 can (15 oz) cooked chickpeas
2 cans (15.25 oz each) sweet whole kernel corn
2 tablespoons olive oil
¼ teaspoon chili flakes
½ teaspoon sumac
Salt
Pepper
1 oz pitted black olives, sliced

1 large red bell pepper, diced
Small bunch cilantro, chopped
3 large hardboiled eggs, shelled and grated

Dressing
1 tablespoon tahini
1 tablespoon lemon juice

Method

In a large frying pan, fry the chickpeas and sweet whole kernel corn in olive oil, together with the chili flakes, sumac, salt, and pepper until golden.

Place in a bowl and incorporate the sliced olives, red pepper, and cilantro.

Mix the dressing ingredients and pour over, tossing well. Decorate with grated egg.

TOMATO GAZPACHO SALAD

SERVES 6–8

Deconstruct your gazpacho, and gain a heavenly salad.

Ingredients

Tomato Salad

10 large tomatoes, sliced or diced or quartered
(your choice)
10 cherry tomatoes (or any other tomatoes
depending on what looks great)

Gazpacho Dressing

¼ cucumber, peeled and sliced

6 baby cherry tomatoes, sliced in half
1 teaspoon fresh basil leaves, chopped
2 spring onions, sliced
1 teaspoon white balsamic vinegar
1 tablespoon olive oil
½ teaspoon garlic puree
Salt

Method

Arrange tomatoes in a shallow dish.

Place all the dressing ingredients in an electric blender and blend. Keep tasting the dressing in case you need to add more basil, garlic, salt, etc.

Pour over the tomatoes.

FISH WITH NO FINGERS

BAKED SALMON FISH CAKES WITH POLENTA FRIES

FISH BLINTZES

MEXICAN SALMON CEVICHE

SEA BASS WITH SALSE VERDE

SEA BREAM STEW

STREET FOOD GEFILTE FISH BITES

STUFFED COCONUT RAINBOW TROUT

SUN-BLUSHED TOMATO & ARTICHOKE-CRUSTED LOIN OF COD

QUICK FISH PÂTÉ

TUNA TATAKI

As young children, the classic fish feast meant three fish fingers (*fish sticks* for our American readers) squeezed between two pillows of thick white bread, plenty of butter, and a dollop of tangy brown sauce. As we got a little older, our tastes broadened to fried gefilte fish, canned salmon cutlets (a Jewish mother's store cupboard savior), or a trip with our grandparents to The Sea Shell (a famous London fish and chip shop where every Jewish family ate) for giant haddock coated in matzo meal that hung off the edge of the dinner plate, accompanied by thick cut fries, pickled onions, and heartburn. However, if a fish wasn't dressed up in batter, matzo meal, or bread crumbs, fish could look a little too fishy. Then, one momentous day, while we were doing our homework, Princess Tracey's mother introduced us to a pot filled with a strange-looking pink dip. She announced it was the latest thing to wash up on our shores, all the way from Greece—Taramasalata. It had a curious smell and an unusual texture; no wonder the Greeks wanted rid of it. However, she assured us it was delicious; after all, it was Princess Pink. We became curious. We took deep breaths and dived in, dipping our pita bread (another Greek treat) to test the waters. We discovered to our delight that it was absolutely delicious; We were finally hooked on fishier fish.

Now began a voyage of discovery. On a family sailing holiday . . . (who are we kidding, we're Jewish, so strike that!) . . . we mean on a vacation spent with both families in Bournemouth, England, with not too much sightseeing, a certain amount of **tchotchke** hunting, and a great deal of *eating* (that's better), fish was brought to the breakfast table—the pungent smell of the daily breakfast catch, smoked kippers swimming in butter. We soon caught on, drizzling kippers with malt vinegar and accompanying them with a portion of triangular toast picked from a silver toast rack, as our neurotic mothers screamed, "WATCH OUT FOR THE FISH BONES." We picked our way through. It was well worth all the effort of dissecting this bony bugger, as we knew it would never be served at home. The only *kippah* we would see were the ones our fathers wore for *shul*, for this fishy variety was far too smelly and our mothers would never be able to decontaminate the house.

As for tuna, it was a delight to discover that it didn't only come in a can, even though a can tuna can be a dieter's best friend. Fresh tuna, however—line caught and dolphin-friendly, of course—is a revelation, the sea's answer to fillet steak (try the Tuna Tataki, page 88). As for Dover sole, the most expensive fish on the menu and therefore the one fish you *never* order on a first date if you want to be asked out on a second, its white, succulent flesh adorned with just a little parsley and butter is worth its weight in gold, which is nearly as much as it costs!

However, there was one fish that was and is a fish too far. Scarier than Jaws, it lies brooding in sliced strips, sometimes swimming in a sea of thick red sludge. This deli monster needs nerves of steel for one to allow it to slither down one's throat: the one and the only *schmaltz herring*! No wonder it's served at *shivas*.

We Princess Promise that there are no schmaltz herring swimming within these pages, but only fresh ideas for serving fabulous, fantastic, flavorsome fish that are smoking!

Tchotchke: Small ornament
Kippah: Jewish male head covering
Shul: Synagogue
Shiva: Jewish mourning period for the dead

BAKED SALMON FISH CAKES WITH POLENTA FRIES

SERVES 6–8

This is the Jewish Princess gourmet answer to fish and chips. Don't forget your condiments—how about a dollop of chrain?

You can always add a bun, lettuce, and mayo to construct your very own salmon fish burger.

Ingredients

Baked Salmon Fish Cakes (Makes 12)
1¼ lb canned red salmon (skinless, boneless, drained)
1 large onion, grated
2 scallions, finely chopped
1 teaspoon fresh ginger, grated (use a zester)
1 tablespoon soy sauce

1 lime, zested and juiced
1 bunch cilantro (approximately 1 tablespoon), finely chopped
2 tablespoons gluten-free self-rising flour
1 large egg, lightly beaten
Salt
Black pepper

Method

Baked Salmon Fish Cakes

Preheat oven to 375°F / 190°C.

Mix all ingredients together and incorporate well. Place on a baking sheet lined with parchment paper.

For a professional look, use a ½-inch ring mold or wet hands and form fish cakes (approximately 1 tablespoon of mixture for each fish cake).

Bake for approximately 20 minutes.

Ingredients

Polenta Fries

1 cup polenta

17 fl oz vegetable stock (1 tablespoon bouillon mixed with water)

1½ tablespoons Parmesan

1 teaspoon Dijon mustard

1 tablespoon butter

1 teaspoon tomato puree

½ teaspoon garlic puree

Black pepper

1 egg, separated

Pinch rosemary

Vegetable oil, for frying

Method

Polenta Fries

Place polenta and vegetable stock in a saucepan. Slowly bring to the boil, stirring occasionally. Bring to a strong simmer and stir until the polenta has thickened to a consistency of heavy porridge, approximately 3 minutes.

Remove from heat, stir in 1 tablespoon of grated Parmesan, Dijon mustard, butter, tomato puree, garlic puree, and black pepper.

Whisk the egg white (reserve the yolk) until stiff, then fold into the polenta mixture.

Flatten out the mixture (I use the heel of my hand) onto a lined baking tray 13 × 9½ × 2 inches, creating a large oblong shape roughly ½-inch thick.

Brush with lightly whisked egg yolk. Sprinkle the remaining Parmesan and a pinch of rosemary.

Cover with another piece of parchment paper and refrigerate for at least 4 hours or preferably overnight.

Cut into thick fries. Heat vegetable oil in a frying pan and shallow fry, turning when golden.

Remove and place on kitchen towels to remove excess grease.

FISH BLINTZES

SERVES 8

Some rules are meant to be broken. This dish may have many ingredients and may take a while to cook, but the taste is so tremendous that you will feel Princess Proud when you bring this to the table.

Cheese sauce is versatile. Once you have mastered this recipe, try it out with cauliflower, macaroni, or vol-au-vents. A good cheese sauce recipe is a must.

Ingredients

Cheese Sauce
2 tablespoons unsalted butter
¼ cup all-purpose flour
1¼ pint full-fat milk
1 good pinch nutmeg
Salt
Black pepper
½ cup Emmental cheese, grated
½ cup mature Cheddar cheese, grated

Pancakes (Makes 16)
2 cups all-purpose flour
2 large eggs
18 fl oz full-fat milk
Unsalted butter, for frying

Filling
2½ tablespoons unsalted butter
2 onions, diced
1 leek, finely diced
4 cups mushrooms, peeled, washed, and sliced
1 lb, 4 oz haddock, sliced lengthways into
    16 pieces
Handful fresh flat-leaf parsley, chopped
Salt
Black pepper

Topping
1¼ cup Emmental cheese, grated

Method

Cheese Sauce

In a saucepan, melt butter. Slowly stir in flour to create a roux—the flour and butter will come together. Keep stirring until you have a good shiny paste.

Remove from heat and slowly add the milk, constantly stirring. Return to heat and stir occasionally until mixture begins to boil.

Lower the heat and gently simmer, stirring occasionally for approximately 10 minutes until the sauce thickens.

Remove from heat. Season with nutmeg, salt, and black pepper.

Stir in cheese until it melts and the sauce is smooth. Check seasoning.

Pancakes

Beat all ingredients together (if you can do this earlier, prepare beforehand and leave in the fridge for a better pancake).

Grease an 8-inch frying pan (wipe away any extra butter). Take a ladleful of mixture and fry until the mixture comes away at the sides and looks dry. Flip over pancake to lightly brown.

Keep going until you have 16 thin pancakes.

Filling

Heat butter in a pan. Fry onions, leeks, and mushrooms in butter until soft and golden, then remove.

To assemble, take a pancake, place a tablespoon of the vegetable mixture a third of the way in, then lay a piece of haddock on top. Sprinkle chopped parsley and season with salt and pepper.

Roll up the pancake and place it, open seam facing down, in an ovenproof dish. Continue until your dish is filled with 16 pancakes.

Cover the pancakes with cheese sauce. Scatter Emmental cheese over the top.

Preheat oven to 375°F / 190°C.

Bake for approximately 30 minutes. Finish the dish under the grill for a further 5 minutes until the cheese is golden brown.

MEXICAN SALMON CEVICHE

SERVES 4

This dish will make you want to salsa the night away.

Ingredients

6 fl oz tomato juice
4 tablespoons lager
1 large scallion, finely diced
2 tablespoons fresh lime juice
1 tablespoon freshly chopped cilantro
1 tablespoon flat leaf parsley
1 teaspoon garlic puree
1 teaspoon finely chopped red chili
1½ oz sliced black olives

Rock salt
Black pepper
12 thin slices sushi-grade salmon, skinless and deboned (ask your fishmonger), or 4 oz per person

Garnish
2 large avocados
1 large lemon, juiced

Method

Mix together all ingredients except the salmon.

Pour over the salmon and refrigerate for a couple of hours.

Remove each slice of salmon from the marinade and place on a serving dish layering with slices of avocado. Add lemon juice to the avocado to prevent discoloration. Pour over remaining marinade and serve.

SEA BASS WITH SALSE VERDE

SERVES 4

A simple Mediterranean dish. Just close your eyes and dream of the beach, then get yourself online and book your flights!

Ingredients

Salsa Verde
3 oz fresh flat-leaf parsley
2 oz fresh mint
2 tablespoons fresh lemon juice
1 tablespoon white wine vinegar
1 tablespoon capers
1½ teaspoons garlic puree
6 anchovy fillets
3 fl oz virgin olive oil
1 lemon zest

Sea Bass
4 sea bass (roughly 12 oz each) left on the bone
   (1 per person)
2 tablespoons virgin olive oil
Salt
Black pepper
4 lemons, sliced

Method

Salsa Verde

In a food processor, blend all ingredients except the lemon zest.

Stir in the lemon zest.

Sea Bass

Preheat oven to 350°F / 180°C.

Score the top of the fish. Massage each fish with virgin olive oil. Season with salt and black pepper. Place lemon slices on the sea bass. Wrap each sea bass in a silver foil parcel and bake for approximately 20 minutes (if the fish is larger, cook it longer).

Remove the fish and place under a hot grill for a few minutes to crisp up the skin. Serve with salsa verde on the side.

SEA BREAM STEW

SERVES 2

This catch of the day is always a winner.

Ingredients

1 large onion, sliced

2 tablespoons olive oil

2 small potatoes, peeled and sliced into rounds approximately ⅓-inch thick

2 large sweet potatoes, peeled and sliced into rounds approximately ⅓-inch thick

1 sea bream, approximately 1 lb

2 large tomatoes, quartered

2 cans (14 oz each) chopped tomatoes

2 oz pitted green olives with herbs and garlic

1 teaspoon garlic puree

½ teaspoon salt

1 teaspoon superfine sugar

1 tablespoon flat-leaf parsley, chopped

Method

Preheat oven to 350°F / 180°C.

Fry onions in olive oil until golden brown.

Cook both types of potatoes in salted boiling water for 3–4 minutes and drain.

Lay the fish in an ovenproof dish.

Place the onions, potatoes, fresh and canned tomatoes, olives, and garlic around the fish. Sprinkle with salt and sugar.

Cover tightly with foil and bake for approximately 20 minutes. Remove the foil, sprinkle with parsley, and bake for a further 5 minutes.

STREET FOOD GEFILTE FISH BITES

MAKES APPROXIMATELY 30

Fried gefilte fish goes "street"!

Ingredients

18 oz white fish, minced (ask your fishmonger)
2 leeks, sliced thinly
½ red onion, diced
1 lime, zested and juiced
1 teaspoon dried parsley
1 large egg
¼ cup fine matzo meal
Salt
Black pepper
2 pints vegetable oil, for frying

Batter
1¼ cup all-purpose whole wheat flour
1½ teaspoons baking powder
5 fl oz full-fat milk
5 fl oz water
Salt
Black pepper

Topping
Plain yogurt
Chives, snipped
Pomegranate seeds

Method

In a large bowl, place the minced fish, leeks, onion, lime zest and juice, parsley, egg, matzo meal, and mix together. Season with salt and black pepper.

Take a teaspoon of the mixture and, using wet hands, form into small balls. Repeat until you have used all the mixture. Leave to one side on a plate.

Heat the oil in a large, shallow frying pan.

Mix the batter ingredients together. Using two spoons, roll the fish balls in the batter and then place in the hot oil. Fry until golden brown and remove with a slotted spoon. Place on kitchen towel to soak up excess oil.

When ready to serve, put 6 on a plate and drizzle with yogurt. Sprinkle over chives and pomegranate seeds.

STUFFED COCONUT RAINBOW TROUT

SERVES 2

A trout worth pouting for.

Ingredients

½ red chili, chopped
4 scallions, diced (the white ends only)
1 teaspoon fresh flat-leaf parsley, chopped
6 tablespoons desiccated coconut
6 tablespoons coconut milk
1 teaspoon fresh ginger, chopped

Rock salt
Black pepper
2 tablespoons fresh lime juice
2 whole trout (approximately 6 oz each),
    gutted and cleaned
1 teaspoon olive oil

Method

Preheat oven to 375°F / 190°C.

Place all ingredients in a blender, except for the trout and olive oil, and mix together.

Place the fish on a sheet of silver foil and stuff the insides with mixture.

Sprinkle a little salt on top of each trout. Score the top of each fish by taking a sharp knife and cutting diagonal lines across.

Wrap the foil tightly around the fish and bake for approximately 20 minutes. If the fish is larger, you will need to allow extra time to cook.

Unwrap the fish and brush with olive oil. Place under a hot grill for approximately 5 minutes to brown the skin.

SUN-BLUSHED TOMATO & ARTICHOKE-CRUSTED LOIN OF COD

SERVES 1

A beautifully colored dish that brings some sunshine to your table.

Ingredients

¼ cup Cheddar cheese, grated
1 oz sundried tomatoes in sunflower oil
1 teaspoon sunflower oil from the tomatoes
1 oz chargrilled artichokes (ready-made)
1 teaspoon fresh basil, shredded

Rock salt
Black pepper
8 oz cod loin
2 tablespoons Cheddar, for topping

Method

Preheat oven to 375°F / 190°C.

Blend all the ingredients together in a food processor except for the cod and Cheddar.

Place the loin of cod in an ovenproof dish. Take the mixture and press onto the top of the cod.

Bake for approximately 20 minutes. Remove from oven. Turn the oven to grill.

Sprinkle the top of the mixture with cheese. Return the dish to the oven and grill for approximately 2 minutes until the cheese has melted and looks golden.

QUICK FISH PÂTÉ

SERVES 4

This one is hors d'easy!

Ingredients

3 smoked mackerel fillets
4 tablespoons sour cream
1 tablespoon horseradish sauce
1 tablespoon capers

2 oz sweet and sour pickles, finely diced
Salt
Black pepper

Method

Mash all ingredients together.

Check seasoning.

TUNA TATAKI

SERVES 4 AS A STARTER

You will be so impressed when you see this dish, you might have to apply for a job at a Michelin-starred restaurant.

Ingredients

Tuna

1 teaspoon Sichuan pepper, crushed with a mortar and pestle

1 oz sesame seeds

1 teaspoon dark soy sauce

9 oz sushi-grade tuna loin (ask your fishmonger)

Pink rock salt

1 teaspoon grated ginger

1 tablespoon walnut oil

Method

Tuna

Mix together Sichuan pepper, sesame seeds, and soy sauce.

Sprinkle the tuna with a little salt, and roll in grated ginger. Roll the tuna in the Sichuan pepper and sesame seed mixture, using your hands to press the seeds into the loin.

Heat the oil in a frying pan until hot. Fry the tuna for 30 seconds, sealing each side, including the ends. The sesame seeds will turn golden. Place the tuna on a dish to rest.

Ingredients

Dressing

2 tablespoons fresh lime juice
Salt
½ teaspoon fresh ginger, grated
½ teaspoon dark soy sauce

1 teaspoon clear honey
1 teaspoon mirin
1 tablespoon olive oil
½ teaspoon superfine sugar

Method

Dressing

Mix all the ingredients together and taste; if you need a little more salt or sugar, simply add.

Ingredients

Salad

6 large radishes, sliced thinly
1 cucumber, sliced with a potato peeler to get the ribbon effect
1 red bell pepper, sliced thinly lengthwise

1 scallion, finely diced
1 small bunch cilantro, chopped
(If you wish to add other salad ingredients, go for it.)

Method

To Serve

Place your salad ingredients on a platter.

Using an electric carving knife, thinly slice the tuna and place on top along the center of the salad.

Spoon the dressing over the tuna and salad.

MEAT THE MAIN EVENT

DUCKILICIOUS CHINESE TURKEY

CHINESE CASHEW CHICKEN

COHEN-TUCKY BAKED CHICKEN

LAYERED PROVENCE LAMB

MELT-IN-THE-MOUTH MEDITERRANEAN LAMB

MIDDLE EASTERN STUFFED QUINOA PEPPERS

PRINCESS 100% BEEF BURGER

PRINCESS TOAD IN THE HOLE

ZA'ATAR CHICKEN WITH COUSCOUS STUFFING

STEAK SHAWARMA

Most Jewish Princesses we know have compiled their meaty menus: Monday mince, Tuesday schnitzel, Wednesday chops, Thursday stew, and of course Friday wouldn't be Friday without a roast chicken or three. On the weekends, meat is generally off the menu unless a **cholent** is sitting in the oven or you are still enjoying leftovers from Friday night (who can resist a chicken sandwich on challah with Piccalilli relish, mustard, mayonnaise, and ketchup?). Sundays might see an occasional roast beef lunch (We stress *occasional*, have you seen the price of Top of the Rib?), but generally Sunday is Deli Day, i.e., bagels for breakfast, lunch, and supper, which is enough carbohydrate to fill you up until the following Sunday, when strangely enough you **challish** for blessed bagels all over again. It's called *tradition*.

Even for the most versatile cook, it is easy to find that one has become stuck in a carnivore culinary rut and that familiarity is breeding contempt. A clue to this is when your children look at their dinner in horror, shake their heads, throw down their cutlery, and moan in unison (it's a talent), "Not Monday Meatballs *again*!"

Princess Tracey's childhood memory of meatballs was when her mother went into hospital on a Monday morning. She was delivering her own extra-large meatball, Tracey's sister. The whole neighborhood went into overdrive and delivered their Monday specialty to her mother's kitchen that very same afternoon, meatballs. They now had a mountain of meatballs in the fridge, which unfortunately were not finished on Monday, Tuesday, Wednesday, or Thursday. On Friday, thank G-d, they were invited out. Princess Tracey thought that was the end of them; and how wrong she was! Saturday night she sat down at the table and they were back, now disguised in a sweet and sour sauce. Mom returned on Sunday, and Princess Tracey will never forget what she said, "Bet you've missed my specialty. Don't worry, tomorrow it's meatballs and rice."

In our opinion it is never too late for a meat makeover (or any other sort of makeover; we are the Jewish Princesses!). So, if you are still relying on ingredients that belong to another century: canned peaches from the seventies; mayonnaise and mango chutney, an eighties marinade must-have; Coca Cola or Pepsi for a nineties beef dish; and if you can't live without Knorr's vegetarian bouillon, it is time to jump into our time machine and warp yourself into the twenty-first century to discover amazing, exciting new recipes. Layered Provence Lamb (page 98), Za'atar Chicken with Couscous Stuffing (page 105), and Princess Toad in the Hole (page 103), to name a few. Using fabulous ingredients from all over the globe (thank G-d for technology and the birth of online shopping) that will really make any night of the week "Meat the Main Event."

Cholent: Meat stew that is cooked overnight
Challish: To want something

DUCKILICIOUS CHINESE TURKEY

SERVES 4

You won't have played fowl as this turkey dish tastes just as good as its cousin, duck, and is a lot easier on your pocket.

Ingredients

2¼ lb turkey leg
7 oz Hoisin sauce
1 teaspoon five spice powder

To Serve
Lettuce leaves
Hoisin sauce
Cucumber, sliced into sticks
Scallions, sliced thinly, approximately 1 inch
    long

Method

Preheat the oven to 350°F / 180°C.

In a large saucepan, place the turkey drumstick and cover with water. Bring to a boil, then place a lid on the pan and poach the turkey for approximately 2½ hours until the meat is falling off the bone. Remove the turkey leg from the saucepan and discard the skin, shred the meat, and throw away the bone.

Mix together hoisin sauce and five spice. Spread the mixture over the meat so that it is evenly coated.

Spread the meat out on a foil-lined roasting tray and bake for approximately 15–20 minutes until the meat is crispy, turning the meat occasionally.

Take a lettuce leaf and spread Hoisin sauce. Fill the lettuce pancake with crispy turkey, cucumber sticks, and scallions.

CHINESE CASHEW CHICKEN

SERVES 4

Who needs takeout menu item number 44 when you can cook number 1?

Ingredients

1 cup cashew nuts

4 boneless chicken breasts, with skin, cut into chunky pieces

3 tablespoons corn flour

1 tablespoon olive oil

1 red bell pepper, diced

1 yellow bell pepper, diced

3 garlic cloves, sliced

1 tablespoon fresh grated ginger

2 fl oz dark soy sauce

2 fl oz mirin

1 tablespoon sherry vinegar

1 tablespoon sweet chili sauce

1 tablespoon superfine sugar

7 fl oz water

Black pepper

5 oz oyster mushrooms, sliced

Method

Place the cashew nuts in a large frying pan and dry fry until golden. Remove the cashews and place to one side.

Toss the chicken in 2 tablespoons corn flour (reserve 1 tablespoon for the sauce).

Coat the pan with the olive oil and fry the chicken, skin side down, until brown, and then turn and continue frying until cooked. Remove the chicken.

Fry the bell peppers until cooked and remove.

Mix together the garlic, ginger, soy sauce, mirin, sherry vinegar, sweet chili sauce, and superfine sugar. Mix water with 1 tablespoon of corn flour to make a paste, and add to the sauce mixture.

In the same frying pan, pour in the mixture and bring to a strong simmer until the sauce has thickened and is glossy.

Add the mushrooms and cook until soft. Season to taste with black pepper.

When ready to serve, gently heat the mushroom sauce, add back the chicken and bell peppers, and cook until the chicken is hot. Finally, toss in the cashew nuts.

COHEN-TUCKY BAKED CHICKEN

SERVES 4–6

Diamond finger-lickin' good!

Ingredients

1 chicken, cut into 8 pieces
Salt
Black pepper
4 large eggs
2 teaspoons garlic paste

1¼ cups fine matzo meal
1 tablespoon paprika
1 teaspoon dried sage
1 bunch flat-leaf parsley, finely chopped
4 tablespoons olive oil

Method

Preheat oven to 375°F / 190°C.

Season chicken with salt and pepper.

Whisk the eggs and add the garlic paste to the eggs.

In a separate flat dish, place the matzo meal, paprika, dried sage, and parsley, and mix together.

Dip each piece of chicken into the egg mixture and then roll in the matzo meal spice combination, covering each piece well.

Then, repeat the process for each piece: double-dip again in egg and then in the matzo meal mixture to create a thicker coating.

Line a flat baking tray with parchment paper. Place each coated piece of chicken onto the parchment. Season the chicken again with salt and pepper.

Put in the oven for approximately 1 hour or until the coating is golden and the chicken is cooked through. If the chicken is large, it will take longer to cook.

To add that extra glistening, crisp layer, use a pastry brush to coat with a fine layer of olive oil and place back in the oven for five minutes.

LAYERED PROVENCE LAMB

SERVES 4

This is definitely a Rustic Fantastic dish, served with red wine from Provence, of course.

Ingredients

2 large onions, diced
2 leeks, diced
4 large carrots, diced
1 can (15 oz) mixed beans salad, rinsed
12 lamb chops (allowing 3 each per person)
1 teaspoon rosemary
6 bay leaves, torn
2 large tomatoes, sliced

5 fl oz Kiddush wine
1 tablespoon stock powder
Rock salt
Black pepper
2 lb potatoes (suitable for roasting), peeled and sliced to approximately ⅓ inch
2 tablespoons vegetable oil

Method

Preheat oven to 300°F / 150°C.

Place onions, leeks, and carrots in the bottom of an oven-to-table dish. Next, add the mixed bean salad.

Add the lamb chops, rosemary, bay leaves, and tomatoes.

Mix together the wine with the stock powder, and pour over. Season with salt and black pepper.

Layer the potatoes over the top. Using a pastry brush, cover the potatoes with vegetable oil. Season the potatoes with a little salt.

Cover the dish with silver foil and cook slowly for approximately 2 hours.

Remove the foil and continue cooking until the potatoes have browned, approximately 30 minutes.

MELT-IN-THE-MOUTH MEDITERRANEAN LAMB

SERVES 6–8

This slow-cooked lamb is so delicious it won't take long to eat.

Ingredients

3 lb, 5 oz cubed lamb
6 tablespoons all-purpose flour
3 tablespoons olive oil
3 red onions, sliced
6 celery sticks, diced
1¼ pints red wine
30 oz tomatoes, chopped
2 teaspoons superfine sugar

2 bouquet garni (a bundle of herbs made from thyme, parsley, bay leaves, and marjoram)
1 teaspoon garlic puree
1 can (15 oz) black olives
Salt
Black pepper
6 bay leaves, torn

Method

Preheat oven to 350°F / 180°C.

Toss the lamb in flour.

Heat olive oil in a large saucepan. Once hot, add the meat, searing the sides until brown. Remove the meat and place in an ovenproof dish.

Fry the onions and celery until soft, and add to the meat. Add the rest of the ingredients to the dish, and place in the oven.

Cook for approximately 2½ hours, basting every half hour with the liquid from the dish.

Remove the bouquet garni before serving.

MIDDLE EASTERN STUFFED QUINOA PEPPERS

SERVES 6

Quinoa is a complete protein, gluten- and cholesterol-free. A healthy and delicious ingredient, it is perfect for your gym buddies.

Ingredients

2 tablespoons olive oil
9 oz minced lamb
1 large red onion, diced
1 teaspoon paprika
1 teaspoon cinnamon
1 teaspoon turmeric
1 teaspoon cumin
1 teaspoon dried cilantro
2 teaspoons garlic puree
1 tablespoon grated fresh ginger
½ cup fresh apricots, chopped (approximately 3 apricots)

½ cup sultanas
½ cup dried cranberries
1 lemon, grated and juiced
Salt
Black pepper
1 cup cooked red and white quinoa (follow instructions on box or buy precooked)
2 large red bell peppers
2 large green bell peppers
2 large orange bell peppers

Method

Preheat oven to 350°F / 180°C.

Place the oil in a large frying pan. Add the rest of the ingredients except for the quinoa and peppers. Cook for approximately 10 minutes, stirring continually.

Add cooked quinoa to the meat mixture.

Slice the tops off the peppers and remove the pips. Fill each pepper with the mixture, and place in an ovenproof dish. Place in the oven to cook for approximately 35 minutes.

PRINCESS 100% BEEF BURGER

MAKES 8 BURGERS

There's the honest burger, the dirty burger, and a gourmet burger; but the best burger of all is the homemade *Princess Burger*.

Ingredients

2¼ lb high quality beef, minced
Rock salt
Black pepper
1 red onion, chopped
1 teaspoon chopped cilantro
1 teaspoon garlic powder
2 tablespoons vegetable oil, for frying

To Serve
8 challah rolls
8 gem lettuce leaves
8 slices pickled cucumber
Condiments of choice

Method

Season meat well with salt and black pepper.

In a mini-blender, place chopped red onion, cilantro, and garlic granules. Pulverize to form a smooth paste.

With your hands, mix the paste into the meat, incorporating well.

Divide the meat into 8 sections and roll each piece into a burger shape. Place on a plate. Cover the burgers and put in the fridge to set for 30 minutes.

When ready to fry, coat each burger thoroughly with oil using a pastry brush to prevent sticking.

Cut the challah rolls in half and coat the insides of the bread with oil.

Heat the frying pan until smoking. Place the meat in the pan. Flatten the burgers a little with a metal spatula, and then leave them alone, frying approximately 4 minutes on each side.

Put the challah rolls flat-side-down in the pan until slightly browned.

Serve the burger in the challah roll with lettuce, pickled cucumber, and condiments of choice.

PRINCESS TOAD IN THE HOLE

WITH WARM ONION & APPLE RELISH

A toad in the hole is a popular British supper dish similar to the delicious American popover. It's served with my hot onion and apple relish, which is guaranteed to turn any frog into a prince with just one bite.

Ingredients

8 chicken sausages
1 teaspoon olive oil
2 tablespoons oil, for coating the dish
2 teaspoons diary-free margarine, melted
1 large onion, diced
10 small tomatoes, sliced

Batter
1 cup all-purpose flour
4 large eggs
10 fl oz water
1 teaspoon English mustard
A small bunch (2 tablespoons) fresh basil, chopped
1 teaspoon thyme
Salt
Black pepper

Method

Preheat oven to 350°F / 180°C.

Brush the sausages with olive oil. Place under the grill and cook them until slightly brown. Remove from the oven and leave to one side.

Put 2 tablespoons of oil in an oven-to-table dish and place in the oven for approximately 10 minutes until the dish is piping hot. Remove and coat the inside of the dish with the melted margarine using a kitchen towel.

Scatter the onions and tomatoes on the bottom of the dish and put in the oven to roast for 30 minutes. While this is cooking, mix the batter ingredients and leave in the fridge.

When the onions and tomatoes are ready, place the browned sausages on top. Whisk the batter ingredients again and pour over the sausages. Return to the oven for another 30 minutes.

Ingredients

Warm Onion & Apple Relish

2 tablespoons olive oil
1 large onion, finely diced
1 teaspoon dairy-free margarine
1 teaspoon English mustard

4 fl oz balsamic vinegar
4 fl oz red wine
1 apple, grated
Salt
Black pepper

Method

In a large frying pan, heat the oil.

Fry the onions for approximately 4 minutes, then add the margarine and continue to fry for approximately 3 minutes until the onions are soft. Add the mustard and continue frying.

Pour in the balsamic vinegar, red wine, and apple. Season to taste.

Cook on high for approximately 5 minutes, stirring continually, until the relish has reduced.

ZA'ATAR CHICKEN WITH COUSCOUS STUFFING

SERVES 4–6

A chicken with a light, tasty stuffing that takes this meat to another level.

Ingredients

Stuffing
½ cup couscous
7 fl oz boiled water
½ teaspoon za'atar
½ red chili, finely chopped
2 sundried tomatoes, finely chopped

4 cherry tomatoes, diced
1 small bunch cilantro or parsley, finely
    chopped
½ lemon, zested and juice
Salt
Black pepper to taste

Chicken
1 whole chicken
Olive oil
Salt

Black pepper
1 chopped onion

Method

Stuffing

Place couscous in a saucepan on low heat and add hot water. Stir continuously for about 1 minute until the water is absorbed. Remove from heat and mix in the other ingredients.

Chicken

Preheat oven to 375°F / 190°C.

Stuff the cavity of your chicken with the couscous mixture. Seal the opening with a piece of scrunched up silver foil to prevent the stuffing from leaking out. Massage the skin of your chicken with olive oil. Season with salt and pepper.

Place the chicken in a roasting tray with chopped onions. Cover with silver foil. Roast for approximately 1 hour with silver foil on.

Remove the foil and roast for a further 45 minutes until golden brown and the juices run clear.

STEAK SHAWARMA

SERVES 2

Raid the spice rack; this is will perfectly spice up your life (or dinner date menu). To test whether the steak is done, use the back of your tongs to feel the steak—soft for rare, firmer and springier for medium, and firm for well done. These steaks are also great when cooked on the barbecue.

Ingredients

2 ribeye steaks (9 oz each)
Salt
Black pepper

Shawarma Spice Paste
½ teaspoon cumin
½ teaspoon dried cilantro

½ teaspoon smoked garlic powder
¼ teaspoon smoked paprika
¼ teaspoon turmeric
¼ teaspoon cayenne pepper
¼ teaspoon ground cinnamon
2 teaspoons vegetable oil, plus extra to fry

Method

Season steaks with salt and black pepper.

In a bowl, mix all the ingredients for the shawarma spice paste. Rub the shawarma paste into the steaks.

Heat a frying pan. When hot, fry the steaks until golden brown. Turn and continue cooking.

When cooked (rare, medium-rare, or well-done), remove and cover with foil. Leave to rest for 3–5 minutes.

VEG OUT

CRÈME FRAÎCHE HOLSTEIN VEGETABLE LATKES

CUBAN SWEETCORN SOUFFLÉ

LEBANESE EGGPLANT & CHICKPEA (GARBANZO BEANS) STEW

LENTIL STEW

MOCK CHOPPED LIVER

PERSIAN SULTANA BROWN RICE

PRINCESS PAD THAI

RED ONION TARTLETS

SPINACH & MUSHROOM STRUDEL

VEGETABLE SPELT & POLENTA PIZZA

There was a time when we could have been accused of being veg-acists, and we weren't the only ones. During our formative cooking years, way back in the 1980s, vegetarians and vegetarian food were as rare as discounted Kobe beef in our circles! When issuing dinner party invitations, if a guest replied, "Yes that's lovely, but I am a vegetarian," our only options were peas, a few potatoes, and maybe a pasta bake, hoping that this would cut the mustard. In those days, grocery stores had very few ready-made veggie meals on the shelf, so there was little chance of decanting one onto your best porcelain plate and trying to pass it off as homemade. Life was tough! Cooking for a vegetarian was simply too much of a Princess Problem. If a vegetarian was invited over once, as far as we were concerned, they were never going to be invited again.

However, once our children decided that veggie was edgy at various stages of their experimental teenage years and jumped on the green bandwagon, it simply wasn't a case of not inviting them for dinner. After all, there were years and years of breakfasts, lunches, teas, dinners . . . *oy ya broccoli*!

We now hold up our manicured hands to these vegetarian crimes. We have served our time and no longer believe vegetarians deserve a nut roasting. We are reformed characters, and if we didn't love chicken soup, roast beef, bolognese, melt-in-the-mouth lamb, and fresh fish so much, we really could step over to the green side.

In today's world, being a vegetarian is as common as tofu; just look around your supermarket where shelves are stocked with a huge variety of exciting vegetarian meals with hardly a nut roast in sight. The vegetarian diet is now so easy to cater for, especially if you compare it to all the other diets that are making the rounds: gluten-free, dairy-free, nut-free . . . what next? *Food-free*?

Enlightenment has shown us that vegetables should not be sidelined; they can be the stars of the show, too. Many great restaurants are catching on to this train of thought and are devoting their menus to incredible vegetarian food. We have been astounded by the wizardry of chefs who create innovative, mouthwatering dishes that make the á la carte menus filled with fish and meats actually seem boring.

Now when cooking in our own kitchens, meat and fish are not always on the menu (by the way, our teenagers didn't last long on their veggie diets; one sniff of chicken soup and they turned). These days our vegetable drawers are full, with a whole crop of fresh, fabulous goodies bursting with vitamins and minerals to create meals that our families can't wait to dig into. And no, we don't provide a shovel.

CRÈME FRAÎCHE HOLSTEIN VEGETABLE LATKES

MAKES 25

Sunday brunch never tasted so great with vegetable *latkes*, you might continue to brunch all week.

Latkes: Potato pancakes

Ingredients

2 lb potatoes (approximately 5 large potatoes), peeled and finely grated

1 large onion, grated

2 large eggs, whisked

1 leek, sliced and diced into small pieces

1 can (15.25 oz) sweet whole kernel corn, drained

1 teaspoon sweet paprika

1 teaspoon garlic granules

¾ cup all-purpose flour, plus a handful for preparation

2 tablespoons crème fraîche

Salt

Black pepper

Oil, for frying

1 egg per person (optional)

Watercress, to decorate

Method

Place potatoes in a colander together with the grated onion. Using your hands, squeeze out as much liquid as you can. Or place a large can on top of the ingredients and squash down to get the same effect. Leave to one side.

In a large bowl, place the potatoes, onion, eggs, leek, sweet corn, paprika, garlic, flour, crème fraîche, salt, and pepper. Mix all the ingredients with a metal spoon.

Sprinkle a large plate with a handful of all-purpose flour. Take a small dessert spoon of the mixture and shape latkes into a flat, round shape. Keep doing this with the rest of the mixture and place the latkes on the floured plate.

Heat a large shallow pan with oil. Fill the pan with the latkes, placed side by side. You will probably have to do two to three batches depending on the size of your pan. Open the windows, put the vent on, put your hair in a towel, and light a candle!

Cook the potato latkes for approximately 5 minutes, turning halfway, until golden brown.

Remove from oil with a slotted spoon and leave to dry on kitchen towels to soak up all the residue oil.

As an optional topping, poach 1 large egg per person. To make poached eggs, bring water to a boil in a large, shallow saucepan. Once it is bubbling, take a whisk and beat the water to create a whirlpool effect. Break the eggs carefully into the water (and not from a great height). Allow it to poach for approximately 3 minutes. Remove the eggs with a slotted spoon.

Decorate with fresh watercress. Season with rock salt and pepper.

CUBAN SWEETCORN SOUFFLÉ

SERVES 8–10

So delicious we could eat the whole thing . . . have we? *We're not telling you!*

Ingredients

2 tablespoons butter
1 tablespoon all-purpose flour
3½ fl oz semi-skimmed milk
6 medium eggs
2 cans (15.25 oz each) sweet whole kernel
    corn, drained

2½ cups grated light mature Cheddar cheese
1 cup grated Gruyere
½ red chili, grated
¼ teaspoon grated nutmeg
Salt
Black pepper

Method

Preheat oven to 350°F / 180°C.

Melt the butter in a saucepan over low heat. Slowly mix in the all-purpose flour.

Whisk in the milk until the mixture thickens. Remove from the heat and leave to cool.

Separate the eggs, reserving the yolks and whites. Whisk the egg yolks one at a time into the milk mixture.

Add the sweet corn, cheese, chili, nutmeg, salt, and black pepper.

Whisk egg whites until they form soft peaks. Then, gently fold into the cheese mixture with a metal spoon.

Grease and flour a 12-inch flan dish. Bake for approximately 30–40 minutes.

LEBANESE EGGPLANT & CHICKPEA (GARBANZO BEANS) STEW

SERVES 6

Once tasted, you cannot leave this alone.

Ingredients

2 eggplants (roughly 1 lb each), sliced and diced

1 tablespoon table salt

10 tablespoons olive oil

2 large onions, peeled and chopped

1 teaspoon ground cinnamon

1 teaspoon brown sugar

1 can (15 oz) chickpeas (garbanzo beans) in water

1 tablespoon clear honey

17 oz passata (sieved tomatoes)

Rock salt

Black pepper

2 fl oz water

Method

Preheat oven to 350°F / 180°C.

Lay out your chopped eggplants on a board and sprinkle salt all over them. Leave for 30 minutes, then rinse with cold water and pat dry with a kitchen towel.

In a large, ovenproof saucepan, add 5 tablespoons of olive oil and fry the onions until translucent. While frying, add the cinnamon and brown sugar.

Add the rinsed eggplants and 5 more tablespoons of olive oil. Fry for approximately 5 minutes.

Add the rest of the ingredients except the water, and season well. Cover and place in the oven.

After 20 minutes, add the water and continue cooking for another 40 minutes.

LENTIL STEW

SERVES 8

This stew is extremely versatile. If you don't add the cheese, this can be served as a side with chicken or lamb; it can also be used with fish. Place on the base of the plate, add the fish and charge a *huge* amount of money—designer handbags are gratefully accepted.

Ingredients

1¼ cups dried Le Puy lentils
2 tablespoons olive oil
2 large onions, finely diced
2 leeks, finely diced
1 tablespoon garlic puree
Salt
Black pepper
1 can (14.28 oz) chopped tomatoes
½ can water (use the tomato can)

1 tablespoon vegetable stock bouillon powder
1 teaspoon herbs de Provence
1 teaspoon sage
7 fl oz vegetable stock
Pinch sugar
1 red chili
Fresh parsley, chopped
Soft goat cheese

Method

Soak lentils overnight. Rinse well with water.

In a saucepan, cover the lentils with water and bring to a boil. Leave for 2 minutes, then remove and rinse again.

In another saucepan, heat olive oil, garlic, onions, and leeks, then fry until soft.

Add the rest of the ingredients except the parsley and cheese. Cook for 20–30 minutes with the lid on.

To serve, add chopped parsley and goat cheese.

MOCK CHOPPED LIVER
SERVES 12 AS A STARTER

This mock chopped liver really works, unlike fake Hermes handbags or Louise Vuitton for that matter. Serve with matzo crackers and pickles.

Ingredients

6 large eggs
6 shallots (10 oz total), chopped (shallots are sweeter than onions, but you can use onions if you prefer)
3 tablespoons vegetable oil
1½ cups walnuts
1 oz salty pretzels

1 oz oat bran flakes
1 can (15 oz) sweet peas, drained and rinsed
1 can (15 oz) cut green beans, drained and rinsed
Salt
Black pepper
2 tablespoons mayonnaise

Method

Bring eggs to a boil in water. Simmer for approximately 10 minutes. Remove the shell by rinsing under cold water and rubbing on kitchen towels. Fry shallots in vegetable oil until brown, turning continually so they don't burn.

Add the rest of ingredients except for mayonnaise in a food processor and blend until you achieve your desired consistency. You can also place them in a large bowl and mix with a hand blender.

Stir in the mayonnaise. Check seasoning.

PERSIAN SULTANA BROWN RICE

SERVES 10

A healthy, and delicious, way to eat rice.

Ingredients

1¾ cups brown basmati rice
3½ fl oz vegetable oil
3 medium onions, diced
10 whole cardamom pods
1¾ pints water (or enough to cover the rice by
    about ½ inch)

1 cup sultanas
1 teaspoon turmeric
1 teaspoon mild curry powder
½ teaspoon rock salt
½ teaspoon garlic granules

Method

Rinse rice thoroughly with cold water.

Place vegetable oil in a large frying pan, and fry onions and cardamom pods until soft.

Add rice and fry until each grain is covered with oil and the rice becomes a little translucent.

Cover with water, approximately ½ inch above the rice. Add sultanas, turmeric, curry powder, salt, and garlic.

Simmer for approximately 40 minutes, until all the water has absorbed into the rice. If the rice starts drying out, add a little more water.

PRINCESS PAD THAI

SERVES 4

This is a really fun meal as everyone can make their own type of Princess Pad Thai depending on the toppings they choose.

Ingredients

1 teaspoon vegetable oil, for frying eggs
2 large eggs, lightly whisked
1 tablespoon tamarind
2 tablespoons light soy sauce
1 tablespoon sweet chili sauce
½ teaspoon sugar
2 tablespoons water
1 tablespoon vegetable oil, for frying pad Thai
2 shallots, finely diced
4 radishes, finely sliced
7 oz tofu, cut into small cubes
11 oz cooked, delicate rice noodles

7 oz bean sprouts
1 oz fresh chives, chopped
1 lime, juiced

Toppings
1 red chili, finely diced
1 oz fresh cilantro, chopped
5 scallions, finely chopped (use only the white ends)
2 oz honey roasted peanuts, blitzed in a food processor

Method

Heat oil in frying pan. Scramble the eggs into small pieces. Remove from heat and leave to one side.

Mix together tamarind, soy sauce, sweet chili sauce, sugar, and water. In a small saucepan, slowly bring the sauce to a boil, then remove and leave to one side for later.

In large wok, heat vegetable oil. Fry shallots until soft. Add the radishes and tofu, and cook for 1 minute.

Add the ready-to-use delicate rice noodles and bean sprouts. Fry in the wok for a further 1 minute, tossing ingredients together.

Pour over the tamarind sauce and incorporate well. Add the chives, scrambled egg pieces, and lime juice, once again making sure all ingredients are well mixed together.

Remove from heat and serve with your choice of toppings.

RED ONION TARTLETS

MAKES 12

Serve warm or cold. As an added beauty benefit, red wine is anti-aging!

Ingredients

3 tablespoons unsalted butter

10 red onions (3 lb, 5 oz), sliced (or buy ready-made)

3½ fl oz balsamic vinegar

⅓ cup superfine sugar

14 fl oz red wine

Salt

Black pepper

All-purpose flour, for rolling out

15 oz (approximately) ready-made short crust pastry

10 mini tartlet pans, greased and floured

Method

Preheat oven to 350°F / 180°C.

In a large frying pan, melt the butter and add the onions. Fry until soft.

Add the balsamic vinegar and continue to fry until liquid has evaporated. Scatter the sugar over the onions.

Pour the wine over the onions and continue to cook until you cannot see any more liquid. Season with salt and black pepper

Scatter a clean surface with flour. Roll out the pastry. Place a tartlet pan on the pastry, and, with a sharp knife, cut around the pan (allowing enough room for the pastry to drop into the pan, about 0.8 inches (2 cm) in diameter, so don't cut near the edges). Do this for all 10 pans.

Place the pastry in the pans and shape with your fingers. Fill the pastry with the red onion mixture to the top.

Place the tartlet pans on a baking tray. Cook for approximately 25 minutes.

When cool, remove each tartlet from its pan and serve with a side salad.

SPINACH & MUSHROOM STRUDEL

SERVES 6

Wonderful for ladies who do eat carbs.

Ingredients

2½ cups mushrooms (or mixed mushrooms of
   your choice), diced
1 tablespoon olive oil
1 teaspoon garlic puree
1 teaspoon sumac
1 lb fresh spinach leaves
2 tablespoons half-fat crème fraîche

¼ teaspoon grated nutmeg
Salt
Black pepper
1 ready-rolled puff pastry sheet (approximately
   12 oz)
1 egg, lightly whisked
1 teaspoon sesame seeds

Method

Fry mushrooms in olive oil with garlic puree and sumac until soft. Add the spinach leaves and let them wilt.

Remove the mixture from the heat and squeeze into a sieve to remove any excess liquid.

Stir in the crème fraîche. Season with nutmeg, salt, and black pepper.

Line a baking sheet with parchment paper. Lay out the pastry and brush the edges with the whisked egg. Reserve any remaining egg.

Spoon the spinach mixture down the center of the pastry and flatten it, leaving a border to stop the filling from oozing out. Then, using the parchment paper, lift the edge of the pastry nearest to you and gently roll up. Use a fork to press and indent the sides to seal the edges.

Mix the remaining egg with sesame seeds and brush over the strudel.

Bake for approximately 40 minutes or until golden brown.

VEGETABLE SPELT & POLENTA PIZZA

SERVES 10

There may be a lot of ingredients, but this spelt loaf looks like a masterpiece—and everyone knows a masterpiece takes a little bit of effort.

Ingredients

1¼ cups stone-ground wholegrain spelt flour
15 fl oz water
1 teaspoon olive oil
1 red onion, diced
1 large red bell pepper, diced
1 teaspoon garlic puree
3 cups button mushrooms, chopped
Salt
Black pepper
½ teaspoon dried rosemary
2 oz semi-dried tomatoes, diced
1 cup pecan nuts

4 large eggs
10 fl oz sour cream
½ cup grated Parmesan
⅔ cup polenta, plus 2 tablespoons polenta for the bottom of the pan

Topping
10 cherry tomatoes, halved
½ teaspoon dried rosemary
½ cup grated Parmesan
Rock salt

Method

Preheat oven to 350°F/ 180°C.

Place the spelt in a saucepan on the stove and cover with the water, stirring occasionally.

When the spelt starts bubbling, turn down the heat and then stir continuously for approximately 3 minutes. The spelt will absorb the water, thicken, and darken in color. Take off the heat and leave to cool.

In a large frying pan, add olive oil, onion, pepper, and garlic. Fry until soft.

Add the mushrooms, salt and pepper, rosemary, sundried tomatoes, and pecan nuts. Continue to fry until the mushrooms are cooked.

In a bowl, whisk the eggs, sour cream, and cheese together.

Add the vegetables, spelt, and polenta, and mix together well.

Grease and line a 12½-inch springform pan. Sprinkle the bottom of the pan with two tablespoons of polenta. Pour ingredients into the pan. Dot cherry tomatoes over the top, dried rosemary, and Parmesan. Scatter with rock salt.

Bake for approximately 1 hour.

VIP "VERY IMPORTANT PAREVE" DESSERTS

APPLE, PEAR & HONEY PUDDING

BAKEWELL TART

BLACKBERRY & APPLE MERINGUE PIE

CHOUX PRINCESS PAREVE PROFITEROLES

COFFEE BEAN ICE CREAM

LAZY LEMON TART

ROSH-A-CHALLAH PUDDING

SCOTTISH FLAPJACK BERRY COBBLER

SPICY FRUIT SALAD

ZABAGLIONE WITH LADYFINGERS

When Moses hiked up the mountain on a forty-day expedition, he returned *schlepping* our dietary laws. He declared we could no longer eat milk with or after meat, but he didn't bring with him a Perfect Princess *pareve* cream, margarine, or dairy-free butter; he obviously couldn't carry anything else. If only he had taken a Jewish Princess with him, maybe this rule would not have been set in stone. We can only imagine what a *begrub* he received as Jewish Princesses turned to each other in horror, saying, "Aren't our lives difficult enough? No hairdresser, no washing machines, and we're *camping*?" We can see their raised shoulders and upturned palms spread wide, complaining of yet another headache coming on, "oy" ringing out in unison across the desert as they beseeched, "What are we going to make as a dairy-free dessert?"

And so a biblical quest began for the Perfect Princess Pareve answer, a search through the centuries in every land across the globe; in every market, supermarket, deli, and store. It wasn't the Holy Grail that Jewish Princesses were *challishing* for; it was far more important than that.

Still today, the quest continues. If we can fly a man to the moon, speak on Facetime to our friends and family all over the globe for *gornischt*, clone sheep, and drive a car that parks itself (most useful), why oh why can't we create a pareve cream that tastes like the real McCoy instead of a chemically enhanced, additive-packaged white liquid that needs a great deal of Princess Pepping Up?

We still believe that one day we will receive the answer to our pareve prayers. But until then, we will have to make the best with what we have to work with. And Jewish Princesses are experts at this. Therefore, for this chapter we have been testing and tasting to produce Princess Pareve desserts that will make not only your family and friends marvel, but Moses as well. If the man himself happens to drop by (but we warn you, Mr. M. might be late battling his way through a sandstorm, getting lost on a mountain, or more likely stuck on the freeway), make sure you have plenty of desserts available.

Schlepping: To haul
Pareve: Dairy-free
Begrub: Giving someone a telling off
Challishing: Wanting something
Gornischt: For nothing

APPLE, PEAR & HONEY PUDDING

SERVES 8

This pudding is Princess Perfect for Rosh Hashanah. Start the New Year with something delicious! Serve with a dollop of whipped pareve cream (which you could flavor with a little honey).

Ingredients

4 pears, peeled and sliced (we use Conference)
4 apples, peeled and sliced (we use Pink Lady)
¾ cup sultanas
2 teaspoons superfine sugar
7 fl oz water (approximately), for poaching the fruit
1¾ cups self-rising flour
¾ cup brown sugar
3½ fl oz corn oil

7 fl oz clear honey
3½ fl oz warm water
2 large eggs
1 teaspoon cinnamon
1 teaspoon ground ginger
1 teaspoon mixed spice
1 teaspoon baking powder
1 teaspoon dairy-free margarine, to grease

Method

Preheat the oven to 350°F / 180°C.

Poach fruit with superfine sugar in water for 10 minutes until soft.

Place the rest of ingredients in a mixer and blend to form a smooth batter.

Grease an oven-to-tableware dish approximately 10½ × 10½ × 2½ inches. Use a slotted spoon to remove the poached fruit from the saucepan. Discard the liquid and place in the oven-to-table dish.

Pour the batter over the fruit. Place the dish in the middle of the oven. Bake for approximately 45 minutes until the pudding is cooked.

Check with a knife by inserting it into pudding. If it comes out clean, your pudding is perfect.

BAKEWELL TART

Who needs Mr. Bakewell and Betty Crocker when you have The Jewish Princesses?

Ingredients

Pastry
Springform tart case (9-inch diameter, 1-inch depth)
2 cups all-purpose flour
1 stick (4 oz) chilled dairy-free margarine
1 tablespoon sieved powdered sugar
1 medium egg
1 teaspoon cold water
Baking beans or uncooked pasta, to weigh down the pastry

Filling
6 oz raspberry jam

3 oz dairy-free margarine
1 medium egg
⅓ cup superfine sugar
1½ cups ground almonds
1 teaspoon almond essence

Topping
½ cup flaked almonds

Frosting
⅓ cup sieved powdered sugar
2 tablespoons hot water

Method

Pastry

Preheat the oven to 325°F / 160°C.

Beat together all ingredients for the pastry, except the water and baking beans or pasta.

Add the cold water to bring the dough together. Wrap in cling wrap and refrigerate for 30 minutes.

Remove and place between 2 pieces of cling wrap. Roll out the dough. It should be larger than your tart case to allow for shrinkage. Remove the top piece of cling wrap. Place the pastry over the tart pan, then remove the other piece of cling wrap.

Push the pastry into the sides of the pan using the cling film, now squished into a ball. Leave any overlap to allow for shrinkage. Place either baking beans or pasta on foil in the bottom of the tart pan. Bake blind for 10 minutes.

Remove from oven and remove the baking beans or pasta baking beans and foil. Return to the oven for a further 5 minutes to let the bottom dry out.

Remove from the oven. Leave to cool. Once cooled, trim the edges.

Filling

Spread the raspberry jam along the bottom of the tart.

In a saucepan, melt the margarine (or use the microwave). Remove from heat.

Stir in the egg, sugar, ground almonds, and almond essence.

Pour the almond mixture over the jam and spread evenly, covering the jam. Sprinkle flaked almonds over the top.

Bake for approximately 30 minutes. Remove from oven and leave to cool.

Frosting

Mix together the powdered sugar and water.

Pipe the frosting in a zig zag pattern over the top.

BLACKBERRY & APPLE MERINGUE PIE

SERVES 8

This pie looks magnificent—and it tastes even better than it looks.

Ingredients

Pie
Flour, for rolling
13 oz ready-rolled short crust pastry, or buy a
    10-inch pie crust
Baking beans or uncooked pasta, to weigh
    down the pastry
1½ tablespoons unsalted butter
¾ cup superfine sugar

18 oz apples (approximately 5), cut into
    chunks (we use Pink Lady)
1 teaspoon vanilla bean extract
11 oz blackberries

Meringue Topping
3 large egg whites
¾ cup superfine sugar

Method

Preheat oven to 350°F / 180°C. Grease an ovenproof flan dish, 9¾ × 2 inches.

On a floured board, roll out the pastry larger than your flan dish to allow for shrinkage. Place the pastry in the flan dish, pressing along the sides with your fingers. Line the bottom of the flan dish with parchment paper and pour in your baking beans or pasta.

Bake blind for 10 minutes, remove from the oven, and take out the baking beans or pasta and parchment paper. Return to the oven for an additional 5 minutes to dry out the bottom of the piecrust.

Remove from the oven and leave to cool. Trim the edges of the pie crust with a sharp knife.

In a frying pan, melt the butter and sugar. Add the apples and vanilla extract. Cook for 15 minutes, turning from time to time.

Place the cooked apples and blackberries in the piecrust, and bake for approximately 25 minutes.

When this is nearly finished, make the meringue. Whisk egg whites until stiff, then slowly add the sugar a teaspoon at a time until stiff and glossy.

Remove the pie from the oven and spread the meringue mixture over. To decorate, swirl the top with a fork.

Bake for approximately 20 minutes.

CHOUX PRINCESS PAREVE PROFITEROLES
MAKES APPROXIMATELY 60

Choux Jewish Princesses can do! Top tips for the choux buns: get all your ingredients weighed and all equipment ready before you begin. Invest in a timer, too. These tips take all the hassle out of this recipe.

Ingredients

Choux buns

10 fl oz cold water
½ cup (4 oz) dairy-free margarine
1 pinch salt
1 pinch superfine sugar

4⅝ oz (1 cup, 1 tablespoon) sieved all-purpose flour
4 large eggs, lightly whisked

Method

Choux buns

Preheat oven to 425°F / 220°C.

Place water, margarine, salt, and sugar in a saucepan. Bring to a strong simmer. As soon as the margarine melts, remove from heat.

Pour in all the flour and beat vigorously with a wooden spoon until the mixture forms a dough (this doesn't take long). Return to a low heat and stir gently for another 2 minutes.

Remove from the heat. Place the dough in a bowl and allow it to cool.

When cool, add the eggs slowly while whisking the mixture. When you have added all the eggs, the mixture will be a smooth, glossy paste.

Put mixture in a piping bag with a round nozzle. Pipe small balls onto a tray covered with a silicone baking mat or parchment paper, allowing space between each.

Place in the oven for 10 minutes, then lower the heat to 350°F / 180°C and continue baking for an additional 25–30 minutes.

Remove from the oven. With a sharp knife, make a small hole at the bottom of the choux bun, and leave to cool.

Ingredients

Filling
14 fl oz dairy-free whip
2 tablespoons Cointreau

Topping
1 cup sieved powdered sugar
2½ tablespoons hot water
1 orange, zested

Decoration
2 oz dark chocolate, melted

Method

Filling

Whisk together cream and Cointreau.

Fill a piping bag and insert the nozzle into the hole in the choux bun and fill it with cream.

Topping

Mix together the topping ingredients until a smooth paste forms.

Dip each choux bun into the frosting and leave to set.

Decoration

Drizzle chocolate over choux buns.

Refrigerate until ready to serve.

COFFEE BEAN ICE CREAM

This recipe is dedicated to our dearest friend Colin, a prince among men and an ice cream aficionado.

Ingredients

Meringues
2 large egg whites
4½ oz superfine sugar
1 tablespoon instant coffee
1 teaspoon hot water

Ice Cream
⅓ cup soft brown sugar
3 medium eggs
10 fl oz pareve whipping cream
3 teaspoons instant coffee
2 teaspoons boiled water
¾ cup chocolate coffee beans

Method

Meringues

Preheat fan oven to 275°F / 135°C.

Whisk egg whites until stiff. Slowly add the sugar.

Mix the instant coffee and water together to form a paste. Fold into the meringue mixture using a metal spoon.

Onto a baking sheet, use a star nozzle to pipe miniature meringues (1-inch rounds).

Bake for approximately 1 hour.

Ice Cream

Whisk sugar and eggs until the mixture resembles whipped cream.

Pour the pareve cream into the mixture. Mix the instant coffee and water to form a paste, and add.

Continue whisking until the mixture thickens. Fold in the chocolate coffee beans.

Place in a container suitable for the freezer (we use a metal bowl) and freeze until set.

When serving, dip the bowl in hot water and turn the ice cream out. Stud with miniature coffee meringues.

LAZY LEMON TART

SERVES 10

When life gives you lemons, make this Lazy Lemon Lovers Tart. Fresh and fabulous, it reminds me of summer in Provence (I have a great imagination!).

Ingredients

Pastry
1 tablespoon vegetable oil, plus extra to grease
1 teaspoon all-purpose flour, to flour
8 filo pastry sheets, approximately 9 × 10 inches
Baking beans, to weigh down the pastry

Lemon Filling
7 fl oz fresh lemon juice (approximately 5 lemons)
4 large eggs
½ cup (4½ oz) dairy-free margarine (room temperature)
1½ cups superfine sugar

Decoration
Sieved powdered sugar

Method

Pastry

Preheat oven to 375°F / 190°C.

Grease and flour a 9½ × 1½-inch springform tart pan (leave 1 tablespoon oil for later).

Lay the first pastry sheet over half the pan and the second sheet over the other half horizontally, overlapping the pastry. Now, lay the third piece of pastry vertically over half the tart pan and the fifth over the other half of the pan, overlapping the pastry.

Brush a thin layer of oil over the pastry.

Lay the fifth piece horizontally over the top and the sixth piece over the other half of the pan, overlapping the pastry. Repeat with the seventh and eighth piece.

Trim the edges of the pastry with scissors to the top of the tart pan; don't worry if it isn't perfect, it adds to the rustic effect. Brush another thin layer of oil over the pastry, making sure you cover the edges.

Take a piece of aluminum foil or parchment paper and place on the bottom of the pastry, covering the sides. Add baking beans and push the beans into the edges of the pan. Place in oven to bake blind for approximately 10 minutes. Remove from oven and leave to cool with baking beans still in. If you can, place a heavy dish over the baking beans to stop the bottom from rising up.

Turn the oven down to 300°F / 150°C.

When the pastry case/parchment paper has cooled, remove the silver foil, baking beans, and the heavy dish.

Lemon Filling

In a bain-marie (a saucepan filled with water a third of the way up, with a heatproof bowl on top), place all the filling ingredients in the bowl on top. Over low heat, use an electric whisk on the first setting (if not, you will get mixture all over the kitchen). Whisk the ingredients (don't worry if they look strange at first). Soon, the mixture will start to thicken. Remove from heat after approximately 7–10 minutes.

Pour the lemon custard into the pastry case and place in the oven for approximately 10 minutes until set. Remove and leave to cool.

Once cool, refrigerate. When ready to serve, decorate with plenty of sieved powdered sugar.

ROSH-A-CHALLAH PUDDING

SERVES 8

Something new and exciting for the new year!

Ingredients

14 oz challah bread, crusts removed and sliced into 0.8-inch slices

3½ tablespoons dairy-free margarine, plus extra to grease

4 tablespoons superfine sugar

3 apples, sliced (we use Pink Ladies)

300 ml dairy-free cream

300 ml soy milk

3 large eggs, lightly whisked

2 tablespoons whisky

1.7 oz superfine sugar

2.8 oz sultanas

Method

Preheat oven to 350°F / 180°C. Grease an ovenproof dish with a little margarine.

Butter the sliced challah on both sides with 2½ tablespoons of margarine, and place the challah in a large bowl.

Melt 1 tablespoon margarine in a frying pan. Add 4 tablespoons superfine sugar and apples. Continue cooking, turning the apples from time to time until they are caramelized.

In a separate bowl, mix together dairy-free cream, soy milk, eggs, whisky, and superfine sugar. Pour the mixture over the challah bread and add half of the sultanas.

When the apples are cooked, pour the challah milk and cream mixture into your ovenproof dish. Add the apples over the top of the challah, and sprinkle in the rest of the sultanas.

Place the ovenproof dish inside a large roasting dish half-filled with water. Place in the middle of the oven. Bake for approximately 30 minutes.

SCOTTISH FLAPJACK BERRY COBBLER

SERVES 8
(GLUTEN- AND DAIRY-FREE)

Och aye the noo, as our Scottish Princesses would say. This dessert is worth donning a Scottish kilt for (Fashion designer Dame Vivienne Westwood makes lovely ones).

Ingredients

3 cups gluten-free oats
½ teaspoon table salt
6 oz dairy-free margarine
4 fl oz golden syrup

1 lb, 11 oz frozen berries
2 tablespoons whisky
½ cup superfine sugar

Method

Preheat oven to 325°F / 160°C.

In a saucepan, mix the oats, salt, and dairy-free margarine. On low heat, stir until the margarine has melted and the mixture forms a paste.

Turn off the heat and stir in the golden syrup.

In an oven-proof dish, 9½ inches in diameter, pour in your frozen berries. Add the whisky and sugar. Over the top, spread a thin layer of the flapjack mixture.

Bake for approximately 30 minutes until golden brown.

SPICY FRUIT SALAD

SERVES 8

You don't need to be in a ski resort to enjoy this dessert, but you can if you want!

Ingredients

10 fl oz Kiddush wine
2 cinnamon sticks
3 tablespoons light brown sugar
3½ fl oz orange juice

11 oz blueberries
8 oz raspberries
14 oz strawberries

Method

Add the wine and cinnamon sticks to a small saucepan and bring to a boil.

Simmer for a couple of minutes and stir in the sugar and orange juice. Leave to cool.

Place the fruit in a serving bowl. Pour the liquid over the fruit and place in the fridge to marinate for at least an hour before serving. You can make the wine marinade the night before to save time if you wish.

ZABAGLIONE WITH LADYFINGERS

SERVES 4–6

Ladyfingers that never need a manicure—perfect to dip into a sophisticated Zabaglione.

> For zabaglione at Passover, just use Kiddush wine instead of Masala wine. **Note:** Ladyfingers are not kosher for Passover.

Ingredients

Zabaglione
4 large egg yolks (as fresh as possible)

⅓ cup superfine sugar
3½ fl oz Masala wine

Method

Zabaglione

Fill a saucepan a quarter of the way with water. Bring to a boil, then turn down to very low simmer.

Put eggs and sugar in a heatproof bowl, then place on top of the saucepan as a bain-marie (ensure that no water touches the bowl at any time). With a hand whisker on high, whisk for 2 minutes.

Slowly add the Masala wine in a steady stream and continue whisking for a further 13 minutes on medium to low heat (the mixture will start thickening from about 8 minutes on, so don't panic). Transfer to serving glasses and eat immediately.

Ingredients

Ladyfingers (makes approximately 20)
3 large eggs, separated
1 teaspoon vanilla extract
⅓ cup superfine sugar
1 pinch salt
¾ cup all-purpose flour

Decoration
1 tablespoon powdered sugar

Method

Ladyfingers

Preheat oven to 325°F / 160°C.

Whisk together the egg yolks, vanilla extract, and sugar until pale.

In a separate bowl, whisk egg whites and salt until stiff peaks form. With a large metal spoon, fold in egg whites, a spoon at a time, into the egg yolk mixture.

Sieve a quarter of the flour over the mixture and fold in. Continue sieving until all the flour is used up.

Line two baking trays with parchment paper. Fill a piping bag with a plain round nozzle with the mixture. Pipe long lines, roughly 0.8 inches (2 cm) wide and 3½ inches (9 cm) long. Leave room between each ladyfinger, as the mixture spreads.

Bake for approximately 10–12 minutes until the ladyfingers are golden brown.

When cool, decorate with plenty of sieved powdered sugar.

CAKE—A SLICE OF HEAVEN

FRUIT & VEGETABLE CAKE

GENOESE SPONGE CAKE

HONEY & GRAND MARNIER ICE CREAM CAKE

ITALIAN ALMOND & LEMON POLENTA CAKE

KUNAFA MIDDLE EASTERN CHEESECAKE

MRS. PLUM CAKE

POPCORN CAKE

PEAR & POPPY SEED CAKE

SULTANA CHEESECAKE

WALNUT CAKE

Who can walk past a patisserie without feeling a tingle, a pull, and the unbearable compulsion to step inside just to take a look? In this sanctuary of sugar, spice, and everything nice, one is transported into a freshly baked world, a child again: ogling, sniffing, and studying every delight; fascinated by the mastery of mille-feuille, its flaky pastry, multicolored frosting, and the call of *cream*. Delicious doughnuts, excellent éclairs, and perfect fruit pastries. Which to choose? This decision takes time, scrutiny, and analysis: will it taste as good as it looks? After all, it is a million-dollar-calorie decision. Generally, the answer is a yes, yes, *yes* (why not opt for all three)? As you can see, bakeries make us very, very excited.

Now, home baking has become highly fashionable (that's why we Jewish Princesses love it). The magic of home baking has swept the globe, from cupcakes to croque-en-bouche. Forget book clubs, spin class, and yoga (actually, don't forget spin class and yoga if you are baking, since you are also bound to be tasting). This baking craze is the new creaming and beating workout, combined with a touch of cake décor. Whatever takes your French fancy—whether minimalist or completely over the top, whether using glitters or sugar paste—anything goes well with a lovely cup of tea.

The brilliant thing about baking is that you can do it on your own or bake with others. Our kids still volunteer to lick the bowl, and they are practically adults! It is wonderful therapy, seeing basic ingredients transform into *cake*. You can bake whenever the mood takes you, day or night (who are we to question). All you need is a bowl, a wooden spoon, and a supply of eggs, flour, butter, and sugar. However, if you do happen to have a KitchenAid® or a Kenwood (and someone to help clear up), this can really put the joy into baking.

To become a member of the baking club, there are no membership fees. However, there are some basic rules to follow. Here are our top ten tips:

1. Find a recipe that speaks to you. We have supplied a whole chapter that will make you ooh and aah.

2. Before you begin, check your pantry to ensure that you have all the ingredients, and please make sure they are not expired! Also, ensure that your eggs are used at room temperature as this allows them to disperse more evenly into the batter. While you are at it, butter must also be removed from the fridge to allow it to soften.

3. Preheat your oven to the correct temperature. Remember, every oven varies slightly—some are hotter than others. Get to know your oven and make the changes accordingly.

4. The recipe will state size of pan. *Do not* be tempted to use another size, or you could end up with cake mixture all over your oven, and you wouldn't want that, would you? However, in case of emergencies, did you know that there are companies who come and dismantle your oven, clean it, and put it back together? Just Google.

5. Grease the pan as the recipe dictates.

6. If you are using a springform pan that has seen better days, it is always advisable to wrap silver foil around the outside bottom half of the pan to prevent leakage, or hit the sales and invest in some brand new kitchen equipment.

7. Weigh everything out precisely. Check that you know how to work your weighing scales, and have a spare battery on hand.

8. If a recipe states dried fruit, for example, sultanas, and you don't like them, you can simply swap out for another dried fruit or even nuts. Just make sure you use exactly the same weight as the recipe states or it will affect the consistency and density of the bake.

9. You don't need an "ology" to bake; however, there is a science involved, so don't be impatient. If the recipe states, "Cream until light and fluffy," don't cut corners or you might not be able to cut into your cake.

10. *Don't* open the oven door too early as your cake will be sure to flop or crack. To test when your cake is done, use a sharp knife or, better still, a kebab stick. If it comes out clean, your cake is cooked.

The joy of cake is not only in the baking but also in the giving. A thank-you present, a well-done congratulations, an I-am-sorry apology, or even just to say, "I love you." You don't have to ice the words on top to send a message. Baking speaks the universal language of *yum*.

FRUIT & VEGETABLE CAKE

GLUTEN- AND LACTOSE-FREE

As an alternative, you can make mini cupcakes. Just reduce the baking time to approximately 20 minutes. You can even serve these little treasures after a meaty meal—fruity, veggie, and full of goodness. Reminder, just check that the baking powder and baking soda you use are gluten-free (if you are worried about intolerances).

Ingredients

6 fl oz sunflower oil, plus extra to grease
5 fl oz golden syrup
3 large eggs
3 large carrots, peeled and grated
1 large red apple, grated
1 cup mixed dried fruit
1⅓ cup soy flour

1 teaspoon baking soda
1 teaspoon baking powder
1 teaspoon cinnamon
1 teaspoon ginger

Decoration
1 tablespoon sieved powdered sugar

Method

Preheat the oven to 350°F / 180°C.

Place the sunflower oil, golden syrup, and eggs in a mixer and blend well.

Add the carrots, apple, fruit, flour, baking soda, baking powder, cinnamon, and ginger. Continue to beat until all the ingredients are blended.

Using some sunflower oil, grease and then line an 8-inch baking pan with parchment paper. Pour ingredients into the cake pan.

Bake for approximately 40–45 minutes.

When cool, remove from cake pan. Dredge with sieved powdered sugar.

GENOESE SPONGE CAKE

This cake is best eaten on the day of baking. It makes a fabulous dessert—so light and fresh we can never refuse a second slice.

Ingredients

Sponge cake

2 tablespoons unsalted butter, plus extra to grease

3½ oz all-purpose flour, plus extra to flour the pan

4 large eggs

3½ oz superfine sugar

1 pinch salt

Method

Sponge cake

Preheat oven to 325°F / 160°C. Melt butter in a microwave or saucepan, and leave to cool.

Grease a 9½-inch cake pan with some butter and flour, and line with parchment paper.

Break eggs into a large heatproof bowl, and add the sugar.

Place the heatproof bowl over a saucepan of water to make a bain-marie (only fill the saucepan by a ⅓ so the bowl doesn't touch the water). Using an electric whisker on high, whisk eggs and sugar for 5 minutes until the mixture is light and fluffy.

Mix the all-purpose flour with the salt. Sieve a third into the mixture. Using a metal spoon, fold in the flour and continue sieving in until you have used the other two thirds.

Pour the cooled, melted butter down the side of the bowl and fold in (don't be heavy-handed).

Pour your mixture into the prepared pan and bake for approximately 25–30 minutes.

Remove, turn out the cake onto a wire rack, and leave to cool.

Ingredients

Fillings

2 tablespoons of your favorite liqueur (we use Tia Marie)
10 fl oz heavy cream
2 tablespoons sieved powdered sugar
2 cups berries, sliced (or other chopped fruit of choice)
½ cup toasted flaked almonds

Method

Fillings

Drizzle the liqueur over the top of the sponge cake.

Whip heavy cream with 1 tablespoon of sieved powdered sugar. Spread the whipped cream mixture over the sponge.

Scatter the berries and toasted almonds over the sponge. Finish with the remaining tablespoon of sieved powdered sugar.

HONEY & GRAND MARNIER ICE CREAM CAKE

SERVES 8–10

A cake that looks as spectacular as it tastes.

Ingredients

1 store-bought dairy-free plain sponge cake
3 tablespoons Grand Marnier
3 large eggs
⅓ cup clear honey

13 fl oz dairy-free whip

Decoration
3 oz honeycomb (store-bought)

Method

Slice the sponge cake (don't make the slices too thin or you will get a soggy bottom). Line the bottom of an 8-inch square springform cake pan with the sliced sponge cake. Pour over Grand Marnier.

Whisk eggs and honey until thick and pale.

In a separate bowl, whisk the dairy-free whip until thick. Turn the whisk down to low and slowly add the egg mixture.

Pour into your pan. Cover and freeze, preferably overnight.

When ready to serve, use a sharp knife and release the sides of the ice cream cake. Place the pan on top of a large can and push the ice cream cake up and out.

Decorate the top with pieces of honeycomb.

ITALIAN ALMOND & LEMON POLENTA CAKE

Polenta makes a Prada-Perfect Italian cake. Delicious, especially when served with a dollop of crème fraîche.

Ingredients

8 oz unsalted butter, softened (plus extra to grease)
8 oz superfine sugar
3 large eggs
2 tablespoons lemon juice

1 lemon, zested
8 oz ground almonds
4½ oz polenta
1 teaspoon baking powder
2 tablespoons flaked almonds

Method

Preheat oven to 325°F / 160°C. Grease a 9½-inch round pan with butter and line with parchment paper.

Cream butter and sugar until pale.

Slowly add the eggs. Continue beating and add the lemon juice and lemon zest.

Add the ground almonds, polenta, and baking powder. Scatter flaked almonds over the top.

Bake for approximately 1 hour.

KUNAFA MIDDLE EASTERN CHEESECAKE

You don't have to be a genie to make this Middle Eastern cheesecake, but it looks and tastes genius.

Ingredients

1½ cups superfine sugar
7 fl oz water
2 tablespoons lemon juice
¼ teaspoon rose water
7 oz butter, melted
12 oz kataifi pastry (shredded filo dough, which can be found in Greek or Middle Eastern delicatessens)

9 oz mascarpone cheese
9 oz cream cheese
2 large egg yolks
¼ cup superfine sugar
1 cup blanched almonds
1 cup chopped pistachios

Method

Preheat oven to 350°F / 180°C.

In a heavy-bottomed saucepan, place sugar, water, and lemon juice. Bring to a boil and then simmer on low heat for approximately 10 minutes or until the liquid has become a syrup. Remove from heat and leave to cool.

When the syrup has cooled, add the rose water and set aside to be used later.

Use a little of the butter to grease an 11-inch springform pan.

In a large bowl, break apart the kataifi pastry until all the shreds are loose. Mix the rest of the melted butter in, using your hands, so the pastry is well coated.

Beat together the mascarpone cheese, cream cheese, egg yolks, and sugar until smooth.

Sprinkle blanched almonds over the bottom of the pan. Take half of the kataifi dough and place over the almonds, pressing it down.

Spread the cheese mixture over the kataifi, using a palette knife so you have an even layer. Take the other half of the kataifi dough and press over the top.

Bake for approximately 30 minutes until golden.

Remove from the oven and sprinkle ground pistachios on the top. Pour the rosewater syrup evenly over the cake. Leave to cool and remove from pan.

MRS. PLUM CAKE

Clue: This cake will be eaten quicker than Mrs. Plum from the board game can work out who done it.

Ingredients

1 cup unsalted butter, softened (plus extra to grease)
1 cup superfine sugar
3 large eggs
3 tablespoons Greek yogurt
1 teaspoon baking powder

1 teaspoon cinnamon
2 cups self-rising flour (plus extra to flour)
4 ripe plums, sliced
1 tablespoon plum jam (if you can't find plum jam, use a red seedless jam)

Method

Preheat oven to 325°F / 160°C.

Cream butter and sugar together with a beater. Beat in eggs one at a time.

Add yogurt, flour, baking powder, and cinnamon. Beat the mixture until smooth.

Grease with more butter and flour a 12 × 6 × 2½-inch loaf pan. Pour in the mixture.

Decorate with sliced plums over the top of the cake (make sure there are plenty).

Bake for approximately 40 minutes.

To check if the cake is baked, push a skewer below the plums into the center. It is done when the skewer comes out clean.

Remove from oven and leave to cool. Turn the cake out onto a wire rack.

Melt the jam in a small saucepan and glaze the top and sides of cake using a pastry brush.

POPCORN CAKE

When you want to butter someone up, make this delicious vanilla buttermilk popcorn cake, a true occasion piece.

Ingredients

9 oz unsalted butter, softened (plus extra to grease)
1¼ cup superfine sugar
4 large eggs
5 fl oz buttermilk
2 teaspoons vanilla extract
2 heaped cups self-rising flour (plus extra to flour)
1 teaspoon baking powder

Frosting
18 oz mascarpone cheese (room temperature)
½ cup butter, softened
1 cup sieved powdered sugar
3 grinds salt

Decoration
2 oz salted popcorn

Method

Preheat oven to 325°F / 160°C.

Cream the butter and sugar. Add the eggs one at a time. Beat in the buttermilk and vanilla extract.

Add the self-rising flour and baking powder. Blend to a smooth mixture.

Using extra butter and flour, grease and flour a 9-inch cake pan. Line with parchment paper. Pour in the mixture.

Bake for approximately 40 minutes until a sharp implement that has been inserted into the middle of the cake comes out clean. Turn out onto a wire rack and leave to cool.

Frosting

Whisk mascarpone in one bowl. Whisk the butter in another. Add both the mascarpone and butter together and gently whisk.

Slowly add the powdered sugar and mix by hand. Finally, add the salt and mix in.

Spread the icing on the cake and refrigerate.

Decoration

Remove your cake. When it is room temperature, decorate with popcorn.

PEAR & POPPY SEED CAKE

A light and fluffy cake, featuring poppy seeds that are used in a unique way.

Ingredients

1¼ cups self-rising flour, plus extra to flour
1 teaspoon baking powder
1½ cups ground almonds
4 small ripe pears (14 oz), finely diced (we use Conference)
1 tablespoon poppy seeds
7 oz unsalted butter, plus extra to grease
¾ cup superfine sugar
1 teaspoon vanilla paste (or good vanilla extract)
3 large eggs

To drizzle
4 tablespoons sieved powdered sugar
1 tablespoon hot water
½ teaspoon poppy seeds

Method

Preheat oven to 350°F / 180°C.

Mix flour with baking powder and ground almonds. Toss in pears and poppy seeds. Leave to one side.

Cream together the butter and sugar. Add the vanilla paste or vanilla extract.

Pour in the eggs one at a time, and continue beating. Fold in the flour and pear mixture.

Using extra butter and flour, grease an 8-inch square baking pan. Pour in batter.

Bake for approximately 45 minutes in the middle of the oven. Remove and leave to cool.

Mix powdered sugar with hot water and stir until smooth. While the cake is in the pan, drizzle the powdered sugar mixture over the top (use your artistic skills) and scatter the poppy seeds over the icing to decorate.

Remove the cake from the pan.

SULTANA CHEESECAKE

This should be renamed "Second Helping Cheesecake," as one slice is never enough.

Ingredients

Base
Butter, to grease
Flour, to flour
6 oz sponge cake (store-bought)

Filling
4 cups full-fat cream cheese
4 large eggs
7 fl oz heavy cream

1 teaspoon vanilla paste
2 tablespoons fresh lemon juice
10 oz superfine sugar
1 oz all-purpose flour
4 oz sultanas

Topping
1 oz sponge cake

Method

Preheat oven to 250°F / 120°C. Grease and flour a round 10-inch springform pan.

Crumble the sponge cake by hand and scatter evenly over the bottom of the pan.

Add cream cheese, eggs, heavy cream, vanilla paste, lemon juice, and sugar in a mixer and beat until smooth.

In a separate bowl, mix the flour and sultanas, then fold into the mixture. This prevents the sultanas from floating to the bottom of the cake.

Pour the mixture into the cake pan. Crumble the remaining sponge cake over the top.

Place in the oven for 50–60 minutes until the edges are set. The middle of the cake should still have a slight wobble when you shake the pan very gently.

WALNUT CAKE

Sometimes an old-fashioned recipe is simply the best; just call it retro chic.

Ingredients

½ cup unsalted butter, softened (plus extra to grease)
1 cup superfine sugar
2 large eggs
1 cup self-rising flour (plus extra to flour)
1 teaspoon baking powder
¾ cup chopped walnuts

Frosting
1 large egg white
1¼ cup sieved powdered sugar
1 tablespoon water

Decoration
5 walnut halves

Method

Preheat oven to 325°F /160°C.

Cream butter and sugar until pale. Add the eggs one at a time.

Mix together the flour and baking powder. Toss in the nuts and make sure they are coated with the flour. Add the flour to the egg mixture and beat until a smooth batter forms.

Grease and flour a loaf pan, 9 × 5 × 3 inches, and line it with parchment paper. Pour in the mixture.

Bake for approximately 30 minutes.

Leave to cool, then turn out onto a wire rack. When completely cool, spread the frosting on the cake.

Frosting and Decoration

Place all the frosting ingredients in a bain-marie (a heatproof bowl over a saucepan with heated water; make sure the bowl does not touch the water). Using an electric whisk, whisk frosting for approximately 5 minutes until it thickens.

With a warm palate knife (dip a palate knife in hot water), ice the top of your cake and decorate with whole walnuts.

COOKIES & TINY TREATS THAT TAKE THE BISCUIT

ALICE'S TOPSY TURVY TEATIME TREATS

APRICOT & PECAN BISCOTTI

CHEESY SAVOURY OAT CAKES

COCONUT & VANILLA MADELEINES

COFFEE & CREAM SANDWICH COOKIES

EGYPTIAN SWEETMEATS (GREAT FOR PASSOVER)

LAVENDER LOVELIES SHORTBREAD

MACAROONS OR MACARONS, THE REAL McCOY

GRANOLA BARS JEWISH PRINCESS STYLE

NUTELLA COOKIE BITES

Just when you thought you had made it around the grocery store and had resisted filling your cart with nosh, you get to the checkout line and there they are: boxes and boxes of cookies on special offer, and what Princess can't resist a special offer? You pop in a few of your son's favorite, then pick up a couple of packages for your daughter. You feel guilty, so your hubby gets a box, and then of course there's the gardener to think about. When you get home, you stash them away in the nosh cupboard, reminding yourself *not to touch* even if you are premenstrual. It's no excuse. A few days go by, and as you are sorting out your son's laundry, tiredly picking it up from his bedroom floor (we know, they are so difficult to train), you spy the empty cartons in his trash. He has eaten his, your daughter's, your hubby's, and even the gardener's!

Of course, a store-brought cookie is vital to have available—not just for your son but also for the window cleaner and occasional handy man who will need something to keep them going with their cup of coffee, or should one say *cups* of coffee. And what Jewish Princess can manage without a packet of Graham Crackers? They are an essential ingredient for the base of a banoffee pie and that family favorite, cheesecake.

However, if you want to hobnob with the best, store-bought cookies won't earn you many brownie points. It will be your cookie barrel of delicious, easy, and amazing homemade cookie recipes that will produce magical mouthfuls of pure indulgence.

This indulgence is taken to new levels when it comes to Princess Passover. All year, you might secretly eat a couple of cookies a week, but when it comes to Passover, the secret cookie eater is outed and in cookie heaven, because these sweet bites make a star appearance at every meal, even breakfast! With few carbs on the menu, cookies step in and save the day—see our Egyptian Sweetmeats (Great for Passover) (page 177).

The rest of the year, homemade cookies are sometimes forgotten about, which is such a shame because they are so quick and easy to make. A homemade cookie is ideal for *noshing* on during a game of cards. They make a perfect teatime treat, or moving-in gift (channel your inner Desperate Housewife and stock up on some gift baskets to present them in), and if you turn up with a plate at a **shiva house** you will add a little sweetness at a sad time.

Homemade cookies may be a little naughty, but at least they are not filled with additives and preservatives so your kids will not turn into cookie monsters.

Noshing: To snack or nibble
Shiva house: Where grieving relatives have prayers for the departed

ALICE'S TOPSY TURVY TEATIME TREATS

MAKES APPROXIMATELY 24

Is it a cookie, is it a cupcake, is it a tart? No, it's Alice's very own work of art!

Ingredients

24 mini cupcake paper cases and a mini cupcake pan (1.2 × 0.9 inches)
2 large egg whites
¾ cup superfine sugar
½ cup unsalted butter, softened

1½ cup all-purpose flour
4 tablespoons strawberry jam
12 whole candied cherries, sliced in halves
Sieved powdered sugar, for decoration

Method

Preheat oven to 350°F / 180°C.

Whisk egg whites until they begin to stiffen, then slowly add the sugar to form a thick white meringue.

In another bowl, beat softened butter until smooth. Add egg whites, alternating with flour, to the butter to form a batter.

Place the batter mixture in a piping bag with a star nozzle. Pipe a small swirl into each cupcake paper case, covering the bottom. Add a little jam in the middle. Pipe the mixture over the top. Add half of a glacé cherry to decorate.

Place in oven for approximately 15 minutes.

Remove and leave to cool. Then decorate with powdered sugar.

APRICOT & PECAN BISCOTTI

MAKES APPROXIMATELY 30

These delicious Italian cookies can be stored up to a month in an airtight container—if they last that long. Go dotty over your biscotti, but try not to eat the lot-y!

Ingredients

3 tablespoons vegetable oil
¾ cup light brown sugar
1 teaspoon almond extract
1 teaspoon vanilla extract
2 eggs

2⅓ cups all-purpose flour, plus extra to flour
¼ teaspoon salt
¾ cup chopped dried apricots
1 cup pecans (broken)
1 tablespoon sieved powdered sugar

Method

Preheat oven to 300°F / 150°C.

Beat together vegetable oil, sugar, almond extract, and vanilla extract until smooth.

Continue to beat in eggs, all-purpose flour, and salt. Fold the apricots and pecans into the mixture with a metal spoon.

When the dough has formed, place on a floured board and divide into 3 equal pieces. With floured hands, roll 1 piece of the dough into a long sausage roughly 10 inches in length. Repeat until all dough has been used. Place each log onto a baking tray lined with parchment paper.

Bake for approximately 25–30 minutes until the dough looks lightly browned and firm to the touch. Take out of the oven and leave to cool.

Using a sharp knife, cut into slices about 0.4 inches thick, and lay the slices on a baking sheet. Bake for approximately a further 15 minutes until dry. Turn out onto a wire rack and leave to cool.

Dredge with sieved powdered sugar.

CHEESY SAVOURY OAT CAKES

MAKES 16

These are delightful to serve with drinks and your favorite toppings; they are yummy topped with cream cheese and roasted peppers, accompanied by a glass of the Pink Stuff, of course!

Ingredients

½ cup unsalted butter, softened
3 oz grated strong cheese (i.e. English Cheddar)
½ teaspoon salt
2 oz oats

¾ cup heaped whole-wheat self-rising flour, plus extra to flour
1 egg yolk
2 tablespoons sour cream
1 teaspoon sesame seeds

Method

Preheat oven to 350°F / 180°C.

Add all the ingredients except the sesame seeds to a bowl, and mix until smooth.

Remove the sticky dough and place onto a floured board. Push into a flat circle roughly ¼-inch thick. Using a 2½-inch cutter, cut out the oat cakes. Place onto a baking tray lined with parchment paper. Since the dough is sticky, we find that a small pallet knife really helps to lift them up.

Decorate with sesame seeds.

Bake for approximately 20–25 minutes until golden. Leave to cool.

COCONUT & VANILLA MADELEINES

MAKES 20

Five-star baking made easy. These are best eaten warm, fresh out of the oven. You will need a madeleine pan.

Ingredients

4¼ oz butter (or dairy-free margarine to be pareve), plus extra to grease

2 medium eggs

½ teaspoon vanilla extract

½ cup desiccated coconut

1 cup sieved powdered sugar, plus extra to decorate

1 cup all-purpose flour

¼ teaspoon baking powder

Butter or margarine, for greasing the tray

Method

Preheat oven to 350°F / 180°C.

Melt butter in microwave or saucepan, and leave to cool.

Whisk eggs for 5 minutes. While continually whisking, add the vanilla extract, desiccated coconut, and sieved powdered sugar. Continue to whisk for another 5 minutes.

Turn down your mixer and add a spoonful of cooled melted butter. Then, add a spoonful of flour mixed with baking powder. Continue to do this until the butter and flour is used up.

Grease the madeleine pan thoroughly with extra butter. Fill each madeleine mold with 1 dessert spoon of the mixture.

Place in the oven and bake for approximately 10 minutes. Turn out immediately onto a wire rack and leave to cool.

Dust with powdered sugar.

COFFEE & CREAM SANDWICH COOKIES

MAKES APPROXIMATELY 20

Who needs store-bought cookies when you can create coffee and cream dreams from scratch?

Ingredients

2¼ cups all-purpose flour, plus extra to flour
¼ cup superfine sugar
6½ oz unsalted butter, softened
1 teaspoon vanilla paste
1½ teaspoons coffee essence
1 tablespoon buttermilk

Vanilla Frosting

3½ tablespoons unsalted butter, softened
1 teaspoon vanilla paste
½ heaped cup sieved white powdered sugar
1 teaspoon hot water
Sieved powdered sugar, for decoration

Method

Preheat oven to 350°F / 180°C.

Place all cookie ingredients into a mixer and beat until a dough has formed.

Flour a board and a rolling pin. Roll out the pastry to approximately ¼-inch thick. Use a 2½ × 1½-inch square cookie cutter and cut out the cookies. Place on a baking sheet covered with parchment paper.

Bake for approximately 15 minutes. Remove and leave to cool on a wire tray.

Vanilla Frosting

Mix the butter with the vanilla paste, then add the sieved powdered sugar and water. Beat until smooth.

With a small palette knife, smooth frosting over 1 cookie and then sandwich together with another cookie. You don't need a lot as the frosting is very sweet.

Decorate with sieved powdered sugar. Once set, put in an airtight container.

EGYPTIAN SWEETMEATS (GREAT FOR PASSOVER)

MAKES APPROXIMATELY 30

A new cookie you will have to add to your Passover repertoire.

Ingredients

3 large egg whites
4 oz superfine sugar
3 cups ground almonds
1 apple (2 oz), grated
2 tablespoons kosher Kiddush wine
1 teaspoon cinnamon

1 tablespoon clear honey
½ cup chopped walnuts

Decoration
4 tablespoons powdered sugar

Method

Preheat oven to 325°F / 160°C.

Whisk egg whites until stiff. Slowly add the sugar.

Add the rest of the ingredients except the walnuts. Then, fold walnuts into the mixture.

On a baking tray lined with parchment paper, roll a tablespoon of mixture into a ball. Continue until all the mixture is used up.

Bake for approximately 10 minutes. Remove and leave to cool.

Once cool, toss in powdered sugar.

LAVENDER LOVELIES SHORTBREAD

MAKES APPROXIMATELY 16

These dainty, delicious teatime treats are perfect for a catch-up with your princess pals. If you want to make these as a petit four to serve with coffee, just make the Lavender Lovelies smaller.

Ingredients

7 oz unsalted butter, softened
½ cup superfine sugar
2 teaspoons lavender extract
2½ cups all-purpose flour, plus extra to flour

1 tablespoon full-fat milk
2 tablespoons sieved powdered sugar, for
  decoration

Method

Preheat oven to 325°F / 160°C.

Cream together butter and sugar until light and fluffy. Add lavender extract.

Mix in the flour a tablespoon at a time, then add the milk to form a dough. Use your hands to bring any remaining mixture together. Remove from your mixer.

On a floured board, take half the dough and roll it out to approximately 2 inches thick. Use a cookie cutter, 3 inches in diameter (dip in flour first before you cut to achieve a clean edge). Repeat with the other half of the dough.

Decorate by pricking the tops of the shortbread or drawing lines—let your artistic talents take a leap.

On a baking tray lined with parchment paper, place the shortbreads, leaving room as they will spread. Bake for approximately 10–12 minutes.

When cool, sprinkle with sieved powdered sugar.

MACAROONS OR MACARONS, THE REAL MCCOY

MAKES APPROXIMATELY 30

It doesn't matter if you say *macaroons* or *macarons*—the trick to making these impressive treats is to have everything weighed out and all equipment ready before you start . . . and maybe a little helper. Then, stay *very* calm. When ready to use, sandwich the macarons together with flavored whipped pareve cream or real whipped heavy cream. You can add fruit, chopped nuts, grated chocolate, etc. Like Mr. Wonka says, just use your *imagination*.

Ingredients

4 oz sieved powdered sugar

4 oz ground almonds

3 oz egg whites, kept at room temperature in separate bowls (from roughly 2 large eggs)

4 oz superfine sugar

1¾ fl oz water

¼ teaspoon coloring of choice

Method

Preheat oven to 275°F / 135°C.

Mix powdered sugar with ground almonds.

Place just *one* egg white in the mixer, but do not whisk yet.

Heat the sugar and water on low heat. Use a wet pastry brush to remove any sugar crystals around the side of the saucepan while the sugar is dissolving.

When the sugar has completely dissolved and is beginning to bubble, start whisking on high the egg white you have placed in your mixer. Meanwhile, keep a close eye on the sugar—you are aiming for a translucent syrupy mixture. If the sugar has turned golden or brown, you have gone too far and this recipe will not work.

When the egg white forms soft peaks, add the food coloring and continue whisking. Turn the mixer down to low, then slowly pour in the sugar mixture. Turn the mixer back up to high and whisk the egg white for approximately 5 minutes, until the meringue is glossy and soft.

While the mixer is doing its work, mix together the other egg white with the powdered sugar and almond mixture until it becomes a smooth paste.

When 5 minutes have elapsed, put the almond paste into the mixer and give it a quick whizz so most of the mixture is incorporated.

Remove and finish by incorporating the mixture by hand. Don't overwork it or the mixture will become too loose and the recipe won't work.

Line a baking tray with parchment paper. Fill a piping bag, using a round nozzle, and pipe the mixture into rounds about 1½ inches in diameter on the baking tray. Leave room between each macaron.

Once you have completed this, bang the trays on a hard surface to remove any air in the meringue mixture. Leave for 20 minutes.

Bake for approximately 15 minutes. Remove from oven and leave to cool.

GRANOLA BARS JEWISH PRINCESS STYLE

MAKES 24

Keep in an airtight container. Why go to a store when you can make these easy delicious granola snacks?

Ingredients

3 cups rolled oats
¾ cup light brown superfine sugar
½ cup pecans
½ cup flaked almonds
5 oz unsalted butter, melted

½ cup dried chopped figs
½ cup sultanas
2 tablespoons golden syrup
1 teaspoon cinnamon

Method

Preheat oven to 350°F / 180°C.

Mix the oats, sugar, and nuts. Spread out on a baking tray.

Bake in the oven until toasted, approximately 20 minutes. Stir the mixture halfway through to allow all of it to toast.

Pour the mixture into a bowl and add the melted butter together with the dried fruit, golden syrup, and cinnamon.

Mix well and pour into a shallow pan lined with baking parchment, approximately 10 × 8 inches. Use the back of a spoon to press the mixture tightly into the baking pan.

Bake for approximately 30 minutes.

When cool, slice into even bars.

NUTELLA COOKIE BITES
MAKES APPROXIMATELY 16

These gluten-free Nutella bites will drive you nutty with desire. If you fancy making these for Passover, just swap the Nutella for Passover Chocolate or Nut Spread.

Ingredients

1½ cups ground almonds
½ cup light muscovado sugar

3 tablespoons Nutella
1 large egg

Method

Preheat oven temperature to 325°F / 160°C.

Mix all the ingredients until a smooth paste is formed.

Line a baking tray with parchment paper. Take a teaspoon of mixture and roll it into a ball. Place on the baking tray. These bites spread, so don't place too close together. Bake for 10–15 minutes.

Remove and place on a wire rack to cool. Store in an airtight container.

COUTURE CHOCOLATE

CHOCOLATE APPLE STRUDEL WITH RUM-SOAKED SULTANAS

DARK CHOCOLATE AMARETTO CAKE

CHOCOLATE GLAZED RING DOUGHNUTS

CHOCOLATE ORANGE CHURROS

HAZELNUT CHOCOLATE VIENNESE KICHELS

HAZELNUT & LIQUEUR TRUFFLES

NAUGHTY PEANUT CHOCOLATE FUDGE BROWNIES

PEAR & CHOCOLATE TART

MILK CHOCOLATE MOUSSE POTS

ROCK ON ROCKY ROAD

Chocolate is a melt-in-the-mouth moment, a fix that can fix anything—so delicious that one bite is never enough. A day just wouldn't be the same without a piece of cocoa confection. Whether hidden under foil or found in a fancy box, so great is its power that it evokes emotions of excitement and pleasure, and that's before one even tastes. Chocolate has always been considered a naughty treat. If you had to give up one thing, could it be chocolate? Thank goodness us Jewish Princesses don't have to do Lent!

People have their own powerful personal preferences: some go nutty over praline, others can't wait to dive into dark, many delight in dairy milk, and for a few all other chocolate pales in comparison when compared to soft, creamy white. The chocolatiers are the wizards, the masters of the art of chocolate creation, conjuring up flavors from classic to outrageous that can make us sing out loud when we sample their chocolate notes: "*Mmmmmm.*"

Chocolate needs love and tender care to keep its freshness, taste, and aroma. Always store in a cool, dark, dry place, away from foods that have strong smells as they are easily absorbed. After all, onion flavored chocolate may be a new chocolate flavor gone too far! (Mind you, with the right chocolatier it could be the best thing since salted caramel.)

The best way to store chocolate, apart from in your mouth, is at a cool temperature, out of sunlight and not next to the radiator. The ideal temperature is between 59F and 63F (15C and 17C), with a relative humidity of less than 50 percent. It doesn't need to be put in the fridge, but, if like in my family you want to keep this a private affair, you could try to keep it under lock and key, or hidden in a safe! If chocolate becomes too hot or too cold, the sugar crystals will rise to the top and a white bloom will appear on its surface. It is still edible, but it won't look its best (however, on a Princess Positive note, more for you!). Getting to understand cocoa percentage in chocolate will help you select the right chocolate to satisfy your cravings. For example, a higher cocoa content makes the chocolate less sweet and more intense. That's why baking chocolate has a higher cocoa percentage, resulting in perfect chocolate cakes. (I admit not all my store of baking chocolate makes it into recipes!)

Top quality artisanal chocolate needs to be savored and not scoffed down in one bite. Like tasting a good wine one needs to inhale the aroma (ahh, gooseberries, apple, orange, Godiva). There can be up to four hundred flavors, known as notes, in one bite, so it is an art to decipher what is in each piece of dark fine chocolate. It can sometimes take the whole bar until you hit upon it.

Our advice: find a quiet corner to indulge. Take note of the color. The darker, the more bitter the flavor will be. If you are used to eating chocolate with a high sugar and low cocoa content, this may taste strange at first, but give your palate time to adjust. Another plus, dark chocolate is actually great for your health (hooray), and it is an antioxidant (hooray, hooray!).

When you break the chocolate, it should have a clean snap. If it doesn't, then the chocolate contains a higher amount of fat. Place a small piece—we reiterate, *small*—onto your tongue and allow it to slowly melt. The intoxicating flavors will provide an intense chocolate hit, then a chocolate high, which can turn into an addiction. So be careful, or you could end up on a therapist's couch sharing chocolate together. Mind you, there are worse things in life to be addicted to—makeup, shoes, handbags, clothes, diamonds . . . *oy*, another Princess Problem.

CHOCOLATE APPLE STRUDEL WITH RUM-SOAKED SULTANAS

SERVES 6

A wonderful dessert best served warm. This is delicious with a scoop or two of ice cream, rum yum!

Ingredients

1 cup sultanas
3 tablespoons rum
1 oz dairy-free margarine, for frying apples
1 lb, 2 oz apples (approximately 6), peeled and chopped (we use Pink Lady)
¼ cup light brown soft sugar

1 teaspoon cinnamon
½ cup toasted flaked almonds
6 sheets filo pastry
2 tablespoons dairy-free margarine, melted
3 oz plain chocolate, grated

Method

Preheat oven to 375°F / 190°C. Place the sultanas in a bowl filled with rum and soak for approximately 2 hours, or overnight, allowing them to plump up.

Melt margarine in a large frying pan and fry the sliced apples for approximately 10 minutes. Mix the apples with sultanas, sugar, cinnamon, and almonds.

Lay one sheet of filo pastry on a baking sheet lined with parchment paper. Brush the filo with a little of the melted margarine. Place another sheet on top and brush again. Repeat until you have used all the pastry.

Spoon the apple mixture down the center of the pastry, leaving roughly 0.8 inches around the edge. Sprinkle the chocolate over the mixture.

Roll up the pastry, using the parchment paper to help, forming a strudel. Brush the top and sides, and seal ends, with remaining margarine.

Bake until golden brown for approximately 25–30 minutes.

DARK CHOCOLATE AMARETTO CAKE

A serious mix of Italian amaretto and dark chocolate, this cake is like a date with Al Pacino . . . you wish!

Ingredients

Base
7 oz amaretto cookies
4 oz unsalted butter, plus extra to grease

Cake
6 oz dark chocolate
9 oz unsalted butter (or dairy-free margarine)
1 cup dark brown sugar

4 large eggs, separated (reserve whites and yolk)
1 cup self-rising flour
2 tablespoons amaretto liqueur

Decoration
1 tablespoon sieved powdered sugar

Method

Base

Preheat oven to 350°F / 180°C. Grease a 9-inch springform pan.

Bash the cookies until a fine crumb. Melt the butter and stir into the cookies. Pour onto the base of the pan, making sure the surface is covered and the crumbs are packed down.

Bake for approximately 5 minutes to set.

Cake

Break up the chocolate into small pieces and melt over a bain-marie (putting a heatproof bowl over a saucepan filled with hot water, making sure the bowl doesn't touch the water).

In a separate bowl, beat the butter and sugar. Add egg yolks one at a time until a smooth paste is formed. Incorporate the flour into the butter mixture and beat. Pour the chocolate into the mixture and continue to beat on a lower setting.

Whisk egg whites until stiff and fold into the cake mixture. Stir in the amaretto.

Pour the mixture over the base and bake for approximately 40 minutes. Leave to cool. When serving, dust with sieved powdered sugar.

CHOCOLATE GLAZED RING DOUGHNUTS

MAKES APPROXIMATELY 13

Best eaten on the day. This is so amazing and scrumptious that it will be Hanukkah every week in your house—just so you can make these.

Ingredients

1½ teaspoons easy bake yeast
4 tablespoons warm water
12 fl oz warm milk
⅓ cup superfine sugar
½ teaspoon salt
½ stick (2 oz) unsalted butter, softened (plus extra to grease)
5½ cups strong white bread flour (plus extra to flour)

2 liters vegetable oil, for frying

Glaze
7 oz dark chocolate
4 tablespoons unsalted butter, softened
2 tablespoons golden syrup

Decoration
Powdered sugar

Method

Mix yeast with warm water and leave to stand until foamy. This takes approximately 5 minutes. Place in a mixer that is fitted with a dough hook.

Add the rest of the ingredients, except the vegetable oil, and mix on low for 2 minutes. Then turn up the mixer to medium for 5 minutes until the ingredients form a soft dough.

Place the dough in a greased bowl and cover with cling wrap. Leave in a warm place for approximately 1 hour, until the dough has doubled in size (we use my airing cupboard).

Remove and flatten the dough on a floured board, using a rolling pin to roll it out, approximately 1-inch thick. Using a 3¼-inch cookie cutter, cut out the dough. Cut out the doughnut holes inside these circles of dough using a 1½-inch cookie cutter. (Keep the holes; they are great to fry over. You can cover them with sugar to create mini doughnuts.)

Place doughnuts on a tray lined with parchment paper. Cover with a tea towel for approximately 20 minutes to let them rest.

Heat vegetable oil until hot, and fry batches of doughnuts, turning halfway through cooking, until golden brown. Place on kitchen towels to remove excess oil.

In a bain-marie—a heated saucepan of water with heatproof bowl resting on top that does not touch the water—place all the glaze ingredients and melt until smooth.

When the doughnuts are cool, dip the tops of the doughnuts into the glaze and smooth with a small palate knife. Sieve powdered sugar over the doughnuts.

CHOCOLATE ORANGE CHURROS

MAKES APPROXIMATELY 16

Churros is a Spanish alternative to Hanukkah doughnuts. It's something fun for dessert or teatime, and even breakfast, for all our Spanish Princesses.

Ingredients

Churros
½ stick (2 oz) dairy-free margarine, melted
7 fl oz boiled water
3 heaped cups whole-wheat self-rising flour
1 large orange, zested
⅓ cup superfine sugar

2 medium eggs, lightly whisked
1¾ pints vegetable oil, for frying

For Dipping
1 cup superfine sugar
2 teaspoons cinnamon

Method

Mix the margarine with boiled water.

In a large bowl, mix together the self-rising flour and orange zest. Add the sugar and eggs.

Beat the boiled water mixture into the flour. Beat vigorously until the dough is smooth. Leave the dough to rest for approximately 10 minutes.

Spoon the dough into a piping bag with a small star-shaped nozzle. Heat the oil in a deep-sided frying pan.

When the oil is hot, pipe strips of the dough into the oil to form churros. Use scissors to cut the end of the dough. Fry until golden brown, turning halfway through cooking. Remove with a slotted spoon and pat away excess oil with kitchen towels.

Mix the sugar and cinnamon. Sprinkle the sugar-cinnamon mixture over the churros. Serve immediately with chocolate sauce.

Ingredients

Chocolate Sauce

5 oz plain chocolate

1 tablespoon Cointreau

6 tablespoons (90 ml) light cream (for pareve, use soy light cream)

2 tablespoons golden syrup

1 tablespoon powdered sugar

Method

Chocolate Sauce

Melt the chocolate in a bain-marie—a heated saucepan of water with heatproof bowl resting on top that does not touch the water. When the chocolate has melted, remove from heat and add the rest of the ingredients. Stir until smooth.

HAZELNUT CHOCOLATE VIENNESE KICHELS

MAKES APPROXIMATELY 40

Hazelnut and chocolate: a marriage made in the Jewish Princess kitchen! When piping the mixture, use your imagination and play with different shapes.

Ingredients

7 oz unsalted butter, softened
5 oz light brown sugar
1 medium egg
¼ teaspoon vanilla extract

7 oz ground hazelnuts
4 oz all-purpose flour
5 oz plain chocolate

Method

Preheat oven to 350°F / 180°C.

Cream butter and sugar until fluffy. Add the egg and continue beating.

Add the vanilla extract. Add the hazelnuts and flour.

Line a baking tray with parchment paper. Fill a piping bag, using a star-shaped nozzle. Pipe circles or lines of the mixture onto the tray.

Bake for approximately 8–10 minutes. Leave to cool before removing from the baking tray.

Melt chocolate over a bain-marie (putting a heatproof bowl over a saucepan filled with hot water, making sure the bowl doesn't touch the water). Take a spoonful of chocolate and drizzle over the Viennese hazelnut circles, or dip the long-shaped kichels at either end and leave to set on a wire rack.

HAZELNUT & LIQUEUR TRUFFLES

MAKES APPROXIMATELY 24

We dare you to only eat one; it's *mission impossible*!

Ingredients

Hazelnut Truffles
5 oz milk chocolate
4 oz Nutella
5 fl oz heavy cream
2 dessertspoons liquid glucose

1 tablespoon unsalted butter, cubed and softened
2 tablespoons vegetable oil
¾ cup chopped hazelnuts

Method

Hazelnut Truffles

Finely chop the milk chocolate and place in a bowl with the Nutella.

In a saucepan, place the heavy cream and liquid glucose. Give it a quick stir. Heat the cream slowly until it is just about to come to the boil.

Remove from the heat and pour over the chocolate and Nutella. Stir until the chocolate and Nutella have melted. Add the cubed butter and mix until completely smooth.

Refrigerate for approximately 30 minutes. Prepare a baking tray lined with parchment paper. Pour vegetable oil into a bowl. Remove the chocolate mixture from the fridge.

Dip your hands into the oil and, using your oiled hands, roll the truffles: take a teaspoon of the mixture and quickly roll into a ball in your hands. Place on the baking sheet. Repeat this process until you have used up all the mixture. Place in the fridge for another 30 minutes.

Remove and roll in the chopped hazelnuts. Refrigerate until set.

Ingredients

Liqueur Truffles
5 fl oz heavy cream
2 dessertspoons liquid glucose
2 tablespoons superfine sugar
5 oz 70 percent dark chocolate

1 tablespoon unsalted butter, cubed and softened
1 teaspoon Grand Marnier
1 teaspoon amaretto
2 tablespoons vegetable oil
2 tablespoons sifted cocoa powder

Method

Liqueur Truffles

In a saucepan, mix together the cream, glucose, and sugar. Heat slowly until the sugar has melted and just before the cream begins to boil. Remove from heat

In a separate bowl, finely chop the chocolate. Pour the cream mixture into the chocolate and stir until it has completely melted. Add the butter and continue stirring until the mixture is completely smooth.

Divide the mixture into 2 bowls. Add a teaspoon of the Grand Marnier to one bowl and amaretto to the other.

Refrigerate for at least 30 minutes. Line a baking tray with parchment paper. Remove the two bowls of truffle mixture from the fridge.

Place vegetable oil in a bowl and dip in your hands to cover them in a little oil. Take a teaspoon of the mixtures and quickly roll into a ball. Place on the baking tray. Repeat this until you have used up all the mixture. Refrigerate again for at least 30 minutes.

Remove and roll in the cocoa powder. Put back on the lined baking tray and return to the fridge until they have completely set. Store these terrific truffles in a cool space.

NAUGHTY PEANUT CHOCOLATE FUDGE BROWNIES

MAKES 12

Enjoy these decadent pieces of paradise. They are delicious with or without peanuts, especially if you don't like them or are allergic.

Ingredients

9 oz dark chocolate
¾ cup heaped all-purpose flour, sieved
½ cup (2 oz) cocoa powder, sieved
4 oz dairy-free unsalted margarine, cubed
1½ cups light brown muscovado sugar

3 large eggs
4 oz dry roasted peanuts (reserve 1 handful for decoration)
Sieved powdered sugar

Method

Preheat oven to 325°F / 160°C. Grease and line an 8-inch shallow square pan with parchment paper (use more parchment than necessary so it overhangs the pan, enabling you to lift out the brownies at a later stage).

Melt the chocolate in a bain-marie (putting a heatproof bowl over a saucepan filled with hot water, making sure the bowl doesn't touch the water).

In a separate bowl, mix the sifted flour, sieved cocoa powder, and butter until smooth.

Add the sugar and eggs, and mix well. Pour in the melted chocolate and nuts, stirring with a metal spoon.

Pour the mixture into the prepared pan and spread evenly with a knife. Bake in the middle of the oven for approximately 25–30 minutes. Insert a knife in the middle—if it comes out clean, your brownies are ready. Leave to cool.

When the giant brownie is cooled, scatter peanuts over the top to decorate. Dredge with powdered sugar.

Once set, lift out the giant brownie from the pan using the extra baking parchment as an aid. Using a sharp knife, cut the giant brownie into small squares or hexagon shapes.

PEAR & CHOCOLATE TART

SERVES 8

A tart you can be proud of.

Ingredients

PASTRY
3 oz dairy-free margarine, plus extra to grease
⅓ cup light brown muscovado sugar
3 large egg yolks

1⅓ cup all-purpose flour
⅓ cup sifted cocoa powder
2 tablespoons room temperature water

Method

Beat together all ingredients except the water. When the mixture resembles breadcrumbs, slowly add the water until the mixture forms a dough.

Wrap in cling film and chill in the fridge for 30 minutes. Remove from the fridge. Between two pieces of cling film, roll out the dough to approximately 0.2 of an inch thick.

Grease a springform tart pan 9½ × 1 inch. Remove the top piece of cling film and turn the pastry over into the pan. Using the cling film to help, press into crevices, then remove the cling film and trim the edges.

Refrigerate until ready to use.

Ingredients

Filling

1½ oz dark chocolate
½ cup (1 stick) dairy-free margarine
½ cup superfine sugar
1 cup ground almonds
¼ cup self-rising flour
2 large eggs

3 small ripe pears (peeled, cored, and cut in half)
1 teaspoon lemon juice
1 handful flaked almonds
1 teaspoon sieved powdered sugar, for decoration

Method

Filling

Preheat oven to 325°F / 160°C.

Melt chocolate over a bain-marie (putting a heatproof bowl over a saucepan filled with hot water, making sure the bowl doesn't touch the water). Leave to one side.

Whisk together dairy-free margarine, sugar, ground almonds, and self-rising flour. Slowly add the eggs.

Sprinkle the pears with lemon juice to prevent discoloration.

Remove the tart case from the fridge. Pour in the franzipan filling. Spoon the melted chocolate over, dotting it around the tart. Take a fork or knife and swirl to create a marbled affect (be gentle so you can still see the white franzipan).

Place the pears around the tart, pushing them into the mixture. Sprinkle the flaked almonds over the top of the tart.

Place in the oven and bake for approximately 35–40 minutes. Leave to cool.

Remove from pan. Decorate with powdered sugar.

MILK CHOCOLATE MOUSSE POTS

SERVES 6

This is a quick and easy dessert that children will adore; it's also the hubby's favorite.

Ingredients

6½ oz milk chocolate

2 large eggs, separated

2 oz (½ stick) unsalted butter, melted

3½ fl oz heavy cream

Method

Melt chocolate in a bain-marie (putting a heatproof bowl over a saucepan filled with hot water, making sure the bowl doesn't touch the water). Remove from heat.

Whisk egg whites until stiff peaks form.

When the chocolate is cooled, add the melted butter, egg yolks, and heavy cream. Gently stir until all ingredients are incorporated. Fold in the egg whites a spoonful at a time.

Pour into espresso cups and refrigerate until ready to serve.

ROCK ON ROCKY ROAD

MAKES APPROXIMATELY 30

Life may sometimes be a bit of a rocky road, but that's what makes it even more delicious.

Ingredients

4½ oz butter, softened
10½ oz dark chocolate, broken
5 tablespoons golden syrup
7 oz graham crackers (if possible buy McVitie's
    Rich Tea Biscuits online as they have a
    better bite)

6 oz mini marshmallows
3½ oz salted peanuts
Powdered sugar, for dusting

Method

Melt the butter, chocolate, and golden syrup in a heavy-based saucepan.

Put the graham crackers into a bag and bash them with a rolling pin. You want bite-sized pieces of the graham crackers. But don't worry if you get crumbs; it adds to the texture.

Place half the graham crackers and marshmallows in a bowl. Pour over half of the butter and chocolate mixture and incorporate.

Add the rest of the ingredients, including the peanuts, and mix until all ingredients have a good coating of the chocolate mixture.

Line a pan with cling wrap, allowing the cling wrap to hang over the edges. Tip the mixture into a shallow square tray. Flatten and spread out with the back of a large spoon. Refrigerate for approximately 4 hours or overnight.

Cut into squares with a sharp knife. Turn it out of the pan and dust with sieved powdered sugar.

EPILOGUE

It has been a fabulous foodie voyage bringing new recipes and mouthwatering food photography to create *The Modern Jewish Table*.

We have laughed, cried, tested, tasted, chucked out, fed families (and our whole street), overloaded on sugar, and even gained a few pounds, oy! But don't worry, it has all been worth it to know that you, our readers, now have a wealth of innovative ideas, top tips, and amazing recipes to go back to time and time again to feed your family and friends. We can't wait for you to receive the oohs and aahs you so rightly deserve when your guests taste that first forkful.

When it comes to us, The Jewish Princesses, it is never goodbye, but always hello. Hello to amazing dishes, hello to keeping traditions alive, and hello to new foodie ideas. You never know, we could be popping by one day to say hello with a slice of pie.

Please keep in touch. We would love to hear from all our fellow Princes and Princesses, whatever part of the world you are in.

WEBSITE: www.thejewishprincesses.com
TWITTER: @jewish_princess
INSTAGRAM: @thejewishprincesses
FACEBOOK: thejewishprincesses
YOUTUBE: The Jewish Princesses
EMAIL: thejewishprincesses@gmail.com

ABOUT THE AUTHORS

GEORGIE TARN & TRACEY FINE
THE JEWISH PRINCESSES

Tracey Fine & Georgie Tarn (The Jewish Princesses) take an upbeat, entertaining, Princess Positive–look on life, family, food, and friendship, bringing fun, style, and a dash of chutzpah to the kitchen. Their energy is infectious, and they reach out to all cultures, sharing the secret of what makes Jewish food so fantastic. Writing from the point of view of a home cook, they believe that if *they* can do it, so can *you*. Having completed two American book tours; appeared on British TV, radio, and press; and given numerous cooking demonstrations, they are the sassy British housewives of Jewish cooking.

ACKNOWLEDGMENTS

From our homes in North London to the mountains of Marbella in Spain and to the excitement of New York and beyond, we have traveled, honing and toning our cookery skills. We kept our tempers while trying to temper chocolate. We became a black belt in the art of rolling sensational sushi and sipping sake. We tackled Thai cuisine and were inspired by the newfound harmony of hot, sweet, sour, and salty flavors—lemon grass, tamarind, and galangal. We fell for a French fancy in the shape of must-have macarons. We got saucy, discovering to our delight how not to curdle custard and how to create one hell of a Hollandaise sauce.

We couldn't have done this on our own. We would like to thank our Queen Mothers, Helen Fine and Sandra Chester, who can still whip up a fabulous meal with just three ingredients: a chef, a credit card, and a dishwasher.

To our fathers, Tony Fine and David Chester, who are now following low-cholesterol diets but who still sneak in the odd piece of coffee walnut cake when the Queen Mothers are out shopping.

To Ratty, Georgie's "Prince Charming" Jeremy Tarn: please remember that every anniversary is a diamond!

To our children who are now master chefs in their own right: Maxwell Fine (for your props advice), Channie Fine (for singing us *X Factor* tunes), Cassie Tarn, (for using your extraordinary makeup skills to rewind the clock), Eden Tarn (for spending your time creating props and sorting out our computer and social media), and Darcy Tarn (for taste-testing and telling us the truth, the whole truth, and nothing but the truth).

To our friends, too many to mention (in case we leave anyone out and it causes a **broigus**). The same applies to all sisters, brothers, sisters-in-law, brothers-in-law, nieces, nephews, cousins, aunties, uncles, and any other members of our family we still talk to.

And, of course, let's not forget Princess the cat, Kizzy the dog, and the new addition to Princess Tracey's family, Mustard the "hot dog" miniature dachshund whom even Princess Georgie might look after one day, if he ever overcomes his incontinence.

Once we had the right skills under our Gucci belts, it was time to get The Jewish Princess brand restyled for our new publisher, Skyhorse Publishing, all the way in the US. A huge thank you to Herman Graf for believing in us; you are welcome for Friday night dinner anytime. It may be a **_schlep,_** but it will be worth it. To Kim Lim, our lovely editor, who appreciates all our wacky ideas. To our publicist Jaidree Braddix: we look forward to seeing our name in our own TV show and a Hollywood film (no pressure!).

We would like to thank Talia Salomon for helping at the Props House (a fantastic day out) and Sue Rowlands for letting us raid her props shed (and what a shed it was). Nicholas Constantinou, for your tech design and patience to help us go boldly into cyber space. We had a makeover and a Princess photo shoot with our photographer, Rupa Nagamootoo (Rupa Photography London), accompanied by food stylist Mandy Thompson (Number 12 Creative). They have made our recipes photographic masterpieces. Thank you *so* much to Helen Tyler and Sue Secher for your emergency washing up skills. What a week of fun and sharing of our food cultures. Thank you, Yakir Zur, for our perfect Princess press picture.

A special thank you to Simon Harrison from Kingdom Creative and his production crew who now know what to do with matzo meal.

We must acknowledge our beautiful Princess agent, Dorie Simmonds, who waved her magic wand and got this book off the ground. We know we drive you **_meshuggah_**, but we are The Jewish Princesses, after all.

Last but never least, we would like to thank all of you, our treasured princess readers. Without you we would never sell a book.

Broigus: A bitter dispute or feud
Schlep: To haul
Meshuggah: Crazy

CONVERSION CHARTS

METRIC AND IMPERIAL CONVERSIONS
(These conversions are rounded for convenience)

Ingredient	Cups/Tablespoons/Teaspoons	Ounces	Grams/Milliliters
Butter	1 cup = 16 tablespoons = 2 sticks	8 ounces	230 grams
Cheese, shredded	1 cup	4 ounces	110 grams
Cream cheese	1 tablespoon	0.5 ounce	14.5 grams
Cornstarch	1 tablespoon	0.3 ounce	8 grams
Flour, all-purpose	1 cup/1 tablespoon	4.5 ounces/0.3 ounce	125 grams/8 grams
Flour, whole wheat	1 cup	4 ounces	120 grams
Fruit, dried	1 cup	4 ounces	120 grams
Fruits or veggies, chopped	1 cup	5 to 7 ounces	145 to 200 grams
Fruits or veggies, puréed	1 cup	8.5 ounces	245 grams
Honey, maple syrup, or corn syrup	1 tablespoon	.75 ounce	20 grams
Liquids: cream, milk, water, or juice	1 cup	8 fluid ounces	240 milliliters
Oats	1 cup	5.5 ounces	150 grams
Salt	1 teaspoon	0.2 ounce	6 grams
Spices: cinnamon, cloves, ginger, or nutmeg (ground)	1 teaspoon	0.2 ounce	5 milliliters
Sugar, brown, firmly packed	1 cup	7 ounces	200 grams
Sugar, white	1 cup/1 tablespoon	7 ounces/0.5 ounce	200 grams/12.5 grams
Vanilla extract	1 teaspoon	0.2 ounce	4 grams

OVEN TEMPERATURES

Fahrenheit	Celsius	Gas Mark
225°	110°	$^1/4$
250°	120°	$^1/2$
275°	140°	1
300°	150°	2
325°	160°	3
350°	180°	4
375°	190°	5
400°	200°	6
425°	220°	7
450°	230°	8

INDEX